UWA

Resilience, Dreams, and Victory – "One Woman's Inspiring Path to Success"

By Lady Edith Ebohon

Copyright © 2025 Lady Edith Ebohon

ISBN: 978-1-917778-30-5

All rights reserved, including the right to reproduce this book, or portions thereof in any form. No part of this text may be reproduced, transmitted, downloaded, decompiled, reverse engineered, or stored, in any form or introduced into any information storage and retrieval system, in any form or by any means, whether electronic or mechanical without the express written permission of the author.

DISCLAIMER

"In keeping with storytelling traditions, this book is a work of fiction. The author created all of the characters, events, and locations mentioned in this work. Any similarities to real people, living or dead, or genuine events are entirely coincidental.

Lady Edith Ebohon
(God's delight)

Dedication

This book is dedicated to my mother, Late Deaconess Christie Apenasomi Iruobe, nee Akagbosu. (04/04/63 – 17/05/17)

My mother, I miss you.
You transitioned and went to be with the Lord exactly a week before my birthday. My heart has been broken since then.
You were an epitome of beauty and grace, a classic woman in all you did. You loved God, your family and books. You are and will always be the embodiment of love, the eternal guardian of my heart. With each passing day, I realize how profoundly your presence shaped the person I have become. You were not just my mother; you were my confidante, my prayer partner, my cheerleader, my guiding light, and my unwavering source of comfort and wisdom.

You taught me life's most important lessons with infinite patience and boundless love. You were always there to mend my wounds, both physical and emotional, and to celebrate my triumphs, no matter how small. You were my source of strength, my solace in times of despair, and the reassuring voice in the darkest of nights.

Your love was as vast as the sky and as deep as the ocean. It was a love that knew no conditions, no boundaries, and no end. Even though you have passed away, your love still lives on within me, a legacy of warmth and kindness that I will carry throughout my days.

In your absence, I have come to realize that a mother's love is not bound by time or space. It transcends the physical world, continuing to shape my journey, offering guidance and comfort even in your absence. Your memory is a beacon of love that continues to light my way.

Though I can no longer hold your hand, your lessons and your love remain etched in my heart, guiding me through life's ups and downs. I carry your spirit within me, and I am grateful for the privilege of being your daughter. You were, and always will be, the most profound influence in my life.

With every passing day, I miss you more, but I take solace in the knowledge that your love endures, and that, in my heart, you are still my mother, my love. One day we shall meet to part no more. Continue to rest in peace and power in the bosom of your maker.

Forever in your debt and bound by your love.
Your daughter,
Imuwahen

About Lady Edith

Lady Edith Ebohon is a magnificent woman, full of compassion and inspiration. She has lived an extraordinary life, wearing several hats with grace and purpose. Lady Edith has many years of experience working as a mental health occupational therapist and she takes delight in making a big difference in the lives of people experiencing psychological issues. With unwavering attention and gentle care, she helps people recover their inner strength and reclaim control of their life. Lady Edith's creative approach mixes her various professional expertise with a degree in business administration combined with marketing, a degree in occupational therapy and a master's degree in leadership. Her ability to bridge the gap between effective management practices and healthcare delivery stems from her diverse skillset, which ensures a thorough and well-rounded approach to patient care.

Lady Edith's fervent enthusiasm extends beyond her professional accomplishments to her charity work. With boundless love for her community, she promotes mental health awareness and the importance of building positive well-being. Her faith in the power of empathy touches the hearts of everyone she meets. Lady Edith's story does not stop there. She is also a passionate church worker who finds solace and spiritual fulfilment in her beliefs. She inspires others with her commitment, spreading love and hope. She loves to pray and believes firmly in the power of change that God can make happen as seen in her personal life. Lady Edith is a wife, nurturing mother, affectionate grandmother, loving daughter, caring sister, kind aunty and loyal friend. With a loving heart, she effortlessly balances the demands of her family and her career, infusing all aspects of her life with unwavering positivity and vigour.

Lady Edith enjoys telling stories of her life, including its many challenges and accomplishments, as well as the many people she has encountered, in order to inspire others to believe in their own ability to heal, empower, and make a meaningful difference in their lives. Her personal story is a testament to the indomitable spirit that is within each of us, as well as a reminder that through love, empathy, and positive energy, we can make the world a better place. Lady Edith believes that her gift is talking, and she likes to talk to motivate all hearers.

Lady Edith believes that the best way to overcome life's challenges is to discover the transformative power of faith and God's love. In a world full of problems and uncertainty, one must cultivate a deep relationship with God. Individuals can find consolation, guidance, and strength via prayer, scripture, and faith in His divine plan. She embraces the serenity that surpasses comprehension, knowing that God is always present, offering the courage and resilience required to endure life's problems. This is the idea behind her charity "changeTHEstory".

Lady Edith is the author of the inspirational book "Life's Golden Gems" and "Am Alone, What Next". She is also the host of the award-winning YouTube shows "Two Minutes Sunday" and "Relationship Tips, Talks, and Tales". She is a multifaceted speaker and media personality who is deeply concerned about mental health issues affecting women and other vulnerable groups. She is available for speaking events worldwide.

<u>Lady Edith Ebohon</u>
#GodsDelight
#JesusBaby
#EnergyQueen
#EnjoymentMinister
#VibeGoddess
#HappinessMinister

Acknowledgements
God
Partner, children, and grandchildren
Family
Church
Fellowships
Friends
All lovers of God and his kingdom

Foreword

Life is a journey marked by moments of resilience, dreams, and victories. Each step along the way tells a story —a story of struggle, hope, love, and triumph. In Resilience, Dreams, and Victory – "One Woman's Inspiring Path to Success," Lady Edith Ebohon paints a vivid portrait of a life lived with purpose, courage, and unwavering faith. Through the story of Uwa, a woman whose spirit shines brightly even in the face of adversity, we are reminded of the power of perseverance and the beauty of chasing one's dreams.

Uwa's journey begins in the ancient Bini kingdom of Nigeria, a place rich in culture and tradition, and takes her across continents to the United Kingdom, where she pursues education, love, and a better future. Her path is not without challenges—cultural adjustments, the ache of homesickness, the balancing act of work and study, and the complexities of love and family. Yet, through it all, Uwa's resilience stands as a testament to the strength of the human spirit. Her story is one of courage, determination, and the unyielding belief that no dream is too big to achieve.

What makes this story so compelling is its authenticity. Lady Edith Ebohon, with her gift for storytelling, brings Uwa to life in a way that feels both intimate and relatable. Uwa is not just a character; she is a reflection of every person who has ever dared to dream, every individual who has ever leaned on faith to navigate life's storms, and every soul who has found strength in the face of adversity. Her struggles are real, her joys are palpable, and her victories are ours to celebrate.

At its heart, this book is a celebration of the human spirit. It is a reminder that no matter how difficult the road may seem, no matter how far the distance between where we are and where we want to be, we have within us the power to overcome. Uwa's story teaches us that resilience is not just about enduring hardships but about finding meaning and strength in the midst of them. It is about holding on to our dreams, even when the world seems intent on pulling them away. And it is about finding victory not just in the big moments, but in the small, everyday acts of courage and love.

Lady Edith Ebohon's own life mirrors the themes she so eloquently explores in this book. As a mental health occupational therapist, a devoted church worker, a loving mother, and a passionate advocate for mental health awareness, she embodies the very essence of resilience and compassion. Her writing is infused with the wisdom of someone who has walked the path she describes, and her voice is one of empathy and encouragement. Through her words, we are reminded that our stories matter, that our struggles are valid, and that our dreams are worth fighting for.

As you read this book, I invite you to immerse yourself in Uwa's world. Let her journey inspire you to reflect on your own path, to celebrate your victories, and to find strength in your challenges. Let her story remind you that no dream is too big, no obstacle too insurmountable, and no heart too broken to heal. And above all, let her resilience, dreams, and victories inspire you to keep moving forward, no matter what life may bring.

This is more than a book; it is a testament to the power of the human spirit. It is a call to believe in ourselves, to trust in the journey, and to embrace the beauty of our own stories. May Uwa's journey inspire you to live your life with courage, love, and unwavering faith.

With gratitude and admiration,
Rev Divine Adeola Abraham
CEO/Founder: Hands of Hope Foundation

CHAPTERS
Chapter 1 – Mehmet
Chapter 2 – Uwa and Joe
Chapter 3 – A Love Beyond Time
Chapter 4 – A Friend in Need
Chapter 5 – A Lying Tongue
Chapter 6 – And She Said Yes
Chapter 7 – Not Again …
Chapter 8 – Please, Sir, Don't Die
Chapter 9 – You Called Me What?
Chapter 10 - A Journey of Self-Discovery
Chapter 11 – Rekindling Love
Chapter 12 – A New Dawn, A New Uwa

Blurb

Chapter 1 – Mehmet

He stood at the door of the office and looked with repulsion at the Africans as they laughed and joked amongst themselves, speaking their language that disgusted him, especially the Nigerians amongst them. He hated the way they used their hands to express themselves, their mannerisms, attitude, loudness and most especially the way they all worked out their butts cleaning the classrooms and the toilets of a horrible secondary school in the Essex area of United Kingdom as if their life depended on that. He gave them that though; they worked hard. His name was Mehmet.

Mehmet originated from Turkey, and he felt he was better than "the Africans", as he liked to call them. However, he especially liked one of them, a simple lady called Uwa. He thought her name was funny and he had a funny way of pronouncing it. She always corrected him, saying my name is UWA not UWI or UWE. Uwa and he were placed on the second floor of the secondary school and they both shared the cleaning of ten classrooms and six toilets. Uwa always seemed to finish before him. When he asked her why she always rushed to finish before time, she replied that she preferred to finish before the school children started arriving to school as she did not like how they were rude and bad mannered. Uwa told him that in Nigeria where she came from, children were polite and when they saw adults, they were respectful. She said it was a Nigerian thing to show courtesy to adults when you saw them in a way of greeting. He had noticed that Uwa herself bent her knees whenever she came in the mornings as she greeted other Nigerians who she said were older than her.

He also found that funny that Uwa would call them uncle, or aunty or sister or brother, when in fact she had told him they were not related.

What a funny bunch of people Africans are, he would respond, and he would laugh at her many jokes about Nigeria and how she missed her family. He likewise told her jokes about Turkey, but it was never as interesting or as funny as hers.

Uwa thrilled him, her smile, her carriage, her voice, and the way she joked and laughed about everything. He liked that she never took life that seriously and took things in her stride. Uwa's voice was the first thing he heard every morning as he walked into the school they cleaned together. She would be singing her Christian chorus. He so loved her voice. Uwa spoke a lot about her religious beliefs. She called herself a born-again Christian, but he always thought that born agains were religious fanatics who were overly zealous, judgmental, and intolerant of others. This belief stemmed from some others he had met in the time he spent in his last job working as a cleaner/porter in a hospital. There he would see these so-called born-again Christians when they prayed, sometimes loudly, shaking their heads and making very funny facial expressions. To them they appeared holy, but to him they looked like clowns. To his shock he would later see them steal bin bags and toilet rolls from the storage room and put them in their bags, something staff were not allowed to take home. He had also observed them to backbite and gossip about one another. But Uwa was different, different in her behaviour as a Nigerian and as a Christian. Mehmet often would say to himself, "Uwa is so authentic, practical, encouraging, and inspiring." He really liked her. He often thought about her when he was at home.

Uwa told him that she came from a family in Nigeria who were well to do, and her parents were paying her school fees as an international student studying business administration at the University of East London. She said she came to study in the UK because the university she was studying in Nigeria closed due to strike actions from the lecturers. Another thing he found funny about Africa was why on earth would lecturers do that? Uwa said for many reasons but mainly due to the poor remuneration they received as wages. Mehmet understood that, as he knew many people who migrated to other countries to seek greener pastures.

Uwa said education was important to her family and as the first child, she must be a graduate. Uwa said her parents and her fiancé sent her money for her accommodation, education, and upkeep but it was never enough when you considered the exchange rate from naira to pounds. She did not always want to burden them with her extra needs and support; that was why she did this part-time cleaning to make ends meet. Unlike him, Mehmet came to the UK for greener pastures. He once told Uwa that his dream was to make enough money to go back to Turkey and open his own shop selling sport wears. Mehmet was a very keen sportsman; he did not play professionally but he loved football and supported Manchester United.

One topic Uwa liked to talk to Mehmet about was about her secondary school. Uwa went to a girls only secondary school in Nigeria. It was in a different city from where her parents lived. One summer day as Uwa and Mehmet sat across from each other at their favourite coffee shop, the aroma of freshly brewed hot chocolate wafting through the air, Uwa's eyes sparkled with enthusiasm as she leaned in to begin a conversation.

Uwa: (excitedly) You know, Mehmet, this hot chocolate reminds me of my secondary school days because I developed the love for hot chocolate from a cocoa powder I used in secondary school called "Milo" and a powdered milk called "Nido".

Mehmet: (curious) Is that so? Milo and Nido? You seem to be rather enthusiastic about your secondary school, and I'm curious to know what makes it so unique.

Uwa: (smiling) The name of my secondary school is Federal Government Girls College, Benin City. I was there for six years, so imagine the impact it had on my life. It was quite an adventure.

Mehmet: (intrigued) Six years? Tell me more about that; it seems like a worthwhile story. I am intrigued to hear more.

Uwa: (stared to feel nostalgic, but happy) Well, it was situated in a different city from where my parents lived, and it is still there actually. It was an all-girls, as in a female only boarding school, and I have to say, those were some of the most influential and best years of my life.

Mehmet: (leaning forward and smiling) That sounds interesting. What was it like studying and living there? I really like the way you say "as in".

Uwa: (thoughtful) There was a strong sense of sisterhood among the girls. There, I met some of my closest friends. Our school was known for discipline and high academic standards. There are a lot of accomplished women who graduated from the school who are still going strong now, many of whom are in my year group.

Mehmet: (impressed) That's incredible. I can imagine the friendships and memories you must have made.

Uwa: (nodding) Absolutely. And the cultural diversity was incredible. Girls from various origins, nationalities, and regions of Nigeria gathered together. It was a melting pot of diverse experiences and ideas.

Mehmet: (curious) Did you board at the school, or did you commute?

Uwa: (reflecting) I boarded there. It was an adjustment at first, being away from my family, but it taught me independence and resilience. We had a matron who was like a mother to us, and she made sure we felt at home. We also had guardians who visited us and provided for our needs. More interestingly it was not uncommon to have a senior student as a "school mother" who provided some sort of guardianship. Uwa said that laughing.

Mehmet: (smiling) It sounds like you had a strong support system there. So did you have a school mother?

Uwa: Yes, I did, and while nodding, Uwa continued and said, and we had some amazing teachers who inspired us. I remember my English teacher, Mrs. Johnson. She made literature come alive. I learnt to read big novels and stories right from my early years in secondary school.

Mehmet: (grinning) So, it is thanks to Mrs. Johnson that you are such a bookworm. You sure still do like reading.

Uwa: (laughing) You could say that. But it was more than just academics. We had inter-house sports competitions, cultural events, and even community service initiatives. It instilled a sense of responsibility and teamwork.

Mehmet: (impressed) It sounds like an enriching experience, Uwa. Your time at Federal Government Girls College sounds like it had a profound impact on you.

Uwa: (gratefully) It did. Those years shaped me in many ways. I wouldn't trade that experience for anything.

Uwa's eyes lit up as she continued her story, leaning in closer to Mehmet.

Uwa: (enthusiastically) You know, Mehmet, what's even more amazing is that my year group from secondary school, we still have contact. We make it a point to have regular meetups. We even have a WhatsApp group and there is always fun and laughter going on there, thanks to technology.

Mehmet: (impressed) That's incredible. You've managed to keep those connections alive all these years?

Uwa: (nodding) Absolutely. We're like a big, extended family. It's not just about the academic years we spent together, but the deep bonds we formed. We've been through so much together, and it's wonderful to have friends who have known you for that long.

Mehmet: (smiling) It must be quite the reunion when you all get together.

Uwa: (grinning) It's more than a reunion; it's a celebration of friendship and sisterhood. We catch up on each other's lives, share stories, and provide support when needed. It's like a support network that's always there.

Mehmet: (thoughtful) It's beautiful to have such enduring friendships. It speaks to the quality of the connections you formed back in school.

Uwa: (appreciative) It really does. I'm grateful for those friendships. They've enriched my life in so many ways.

Mehmet: (warmly) It's clear how much those years at your secondary school mean to you, Uwa. I'm glad you have such wonderful memories and lasting connections from that time.

Uwa: (grateful) Thank you, Mehmet. It's a part of my life that I hold dear, and I'm glad I could share it with you.

Uwa also told him she was engaged to a man from Nigerian descent but from a different tribe to her. She explained how though Nigeria had three main tribes – Yoruba, Ibo, and Hausa – she was from a minority tribe – Bini. She said her fiancé was Yoruba. He was a banker in Nigeria, and they were very much in love and hoped to get married in the next two to three years. His name was Joe. Mehmet heard Uwa on some mornings whilst she mopped the classroom floor speaking to her darling and the smile on her face was so beautiful, one could tell she was happy otherwise he would have asked her out himself. He wished she were single as he would love to hug and wrap her in his arms, but he respected her too much to do anything to jeopardize their friendship. Mehmet never mixed with the other Africans; they were all so unlike Uwa. He wanted to leave the job but stayed on because of Uwa. He liked seeing her every morning.

To Mehmet's surprise, one day Uwa did not turn up for work and neither did she the next day and the next day, and in fact the whole week. It made work unpleasant for him. The following week, she still did not turn up. Mehmet was gutted. He was unhappy that all the times he had known Uwa he'd never taken her phone number. As he did not speak to the other workers, he could not ask them why Uwa had not been coming to work. After three weeks, Uwa came back and she told Mehmet that she had gone to Lagos Nigeria to visit her fiancé for two weeks. Even though it was not school holidays, she had to go. She said her fiancé wanted them to do a registry wedding before they did their white and traditional wedding to seal the bond between them. It was also the Valentine season and they had wanted to spend it together as lovers would. Uwa was now officially a married woman.

Mehmet said to himself that Uwa's fiancé was right to do so otherwise Uwa might be swept off her feet by another man in the UK, as her fiancé and she lived far apart. Uwa was definitely a golden girl, one you could never miss in any gathering. He said thinking for himself as the first person who would have loved to ask Uwa to be his girlfriend. The lost possibility brought a sad sigh to his lips.

Uwa also gave Mehmet another surprise news. She had gotten a new job working in a shop. It paid better than the £50 a week they got for doing the cleaning job. Uwa explained that she was always so tired getting up so early, doing cleaning and going for her lectures afterwards. She preferred to go for her lectures and work on days she had no lectures and at weekends. She said more so the new job pays better than the cleaning. Uwa said that week that Friday was her last day. Mehmet was gutted she was leaving, but he understood, as he had a second job he did after the cleaning job in the morning. Mehmet was very frugal and tried to put away as much money as he could for his business. He cut back on frivolous spending, stuck to his budget, and saved a regular amount of money. Every dime he saved got him one step closer to his goal, and he knew it.

On the Friday, Uwa's last day, Mehmet said goodbye to Uwa with tears in his eyes. He gave her a beautiful ornament as a parting gift and kissed her on both cheeks as it was the customary Turkish tradition when greeting friends. They did not exchange numbers; after all, she was now a married woman.

They never met again.

Chapter 2 – Uwa and Joe

This was 1995. A 22-year-old young lady from the beautiful ancient Bini kingdom, Edo state, Nigeria named Uwa looked up at the beautiful sunset sitting on the bench in a park near her new home in the United Kingdom. Uwa had left her home country, Nigeria, her parents, siblings, friends, and all she knew and relocated to the United Kingdom as an international student to pursue her studies. Uwa also left a special person in Nigeria when she came to UK: her fiancé, Joe. Uwa was the first born of her parents. Her mother was a beautiful woman, elegant, lover of God, her family, people, and books. Uwa and her mother were very close; as her mother would often say that Uwa and her had grown up together, and they shared a very special bond. What was also special about Uwa was that she had two fathers: her biological father who was a very successful barrister and solicitor, and a stepfather who was highly educated, very involved in her up bringing, a great provider and a lover of God who she lived with and grew up with. He was loving, caring, supportive and gave her most learnings she had from life with inspiration and impactful knowledge. Uwa had siblings from her father's side, but she never fully related to them, and she lived mainly with her mum, her stepdad and five siblings, all who were birthed by her mother. Uwa's siblings from her mother consisted of three sisters and two brothers. They were close and united. They all loved Uwa and respected her as the eldest; they were proud of her, and over the coming years in Uwa's life they were her main support system. They were always there to provide love and support.

Uwa was studying in a well-known prestigious university in Nigeria when an issue over the pay for lecturers and university staff ensued. This resulted in strike actions, the university closing temporarily, and all students were sent home till further notice. This impacted on her being able to complete her education. Her desire to continue her studies burned brightly within her as she believed that education was the key to unlocking a brighter future. Uwa was lucky that her family were able to send her to the UK do her schooling. She worked hard over the next two years and qualified with a degree in business administration combined with marketing.

Every day, Uwa would wake up before dawn, slipping out of the tiny apartment she shared with several other individuals. She would do odd jobs, attend lectures, go to the library to devour books, seeking knowledge and self-improvement. There, in the quiet with the smell of ancient books and whispers, she discovered peace in her new life. Late at night, she would return home and, on most occasions, sob her way to sleep. She longed for the familiarity of home and all its comforts, including her fiancé Joe, her family, her favourite TV shows, and proper Nigerian homemade food, Uwa sure did miss her mum's cooking. Uwa missed "suya" the most, a Nigerian street meal of grilled beef, chicken, lamb, or goat seasoned with various spices and cooked to perfection. The flavours melted in her mind and were always a happy moment for her. Uwa's faith in God gave her the courage and optimism she needed during those difficult days. Uwa learnt to pray and seek comfort from God's words.

Uwa loved the weekends. As she did not need to wake early on Saturdays, she would have a lie in, then she would go to the library and in the evenings, she would attend choir practice in her church. Uwa would sometimes visit her aunty, who she fondly called Aunty B, and her family. Aunty B and Uwa's mum were cousins and Aunty B had lived with Uwa's mum, dad and Uwa in her teenage years. Aunty B made the most delicious meals ever and she would often give Uwa food to take home. This made Uwa miss home even more, Aunty B and Uwa's mum had similar ways of cooking. Uwa especially liked Aunty B's stew that consisted of so much meat, chicken and fish which she would eat with rice and fried plantain. Aunty B had a caring husband who would give Uwa some money as pocket money when she left their home. Aunty B and her husband had two precious daughters whom Uwa loved a lot. Uwa had other family members she visited too from time to time. She attended a Pentecostal church, and she loved singing and dancing. She loved the bible and would spend hours reading it and learning verses off by heart. Uwa always made a long phone call to her family every Sunday evening and she looked forward to that.

Uwa cherished the beautiful relationship she shared with her mother. She was the first born of parents, and the first born in her culture was very well respected. They were more than just family; they were confidantes, friends, prayer partner, gist partner and much more. They had an unbreakable bond that tied their hearts together. They spoke on the phone nearly every day, despite the difference in time and distance. Whatever they talked about—the ordinary events of the day, the newest rumours in the family, or their deepest, darkest secrets—it made no difference. The sound of their laughing, the familiarity of their voices, and the assurance that they could always rely on one another were what truly counted. The soothing pace of her mother's voice would comfort Uwa's worries whenever she needed encouragement, advice, or just someone to talk to about her feelings. She could sense the love and support from her mother's voice. The strength of family bonds was firm, and this bond served as a reassuring reminder that they would always be by one other's side no matter where life led them.

Naturally, Uwa also cherished conversing with her fiancé Joe; the love between the two of them knew no bounds, not even physical distance. Uwa and Joe talked every day. They stayed connected through social media, instant messaging, and other communication means that they found which kept their love alive and strong. Those late-night chats, virtual goodnights, and shared joys and sorrows were cherished by Uwa. Joe assured her time and time again that they would be a happy couple, whether that meant he would go to the UK to be with her once she finished school there or she returned to Nigeria. While that was happening, he made sure to take care of Uwa and build a lovely future for them. Because of this, she looked forward to talking to her lover Joe late at night. She would find a comfortable spot in her living room and hold her phone tightly, as if it were her lifeline. Uwa would then tap Joe's name on her phone, eagerly anticipating the ringtone and the sound of his voice. "Hey, Uwa," Joe would say in the most charming voice. Have you had a good day? Joe would always ask. She felt comfort and couldn't help but smile. "Joe, it's always better when I'm talking to you," she would reply.

One day whilst they talked on phone, Joe said, "Uwa, I have been thinking. We should get married. I think we can do that now that you have almost completed your studies. My other decision is that I will join you and we will live and raise our children in the UK."

Uwa held her breath as Joe's words hung in the air. The gravity of his words washed over her, and for a moment, time seemed to stand still. "Joe," Uwa said, "you've given me the greatest gift with those words. I can't imagine a more beautiful future than one with you. To think of us getting married and building a life together—it's a dream come true." Joe and Uwa's shared future grew clearer with every conversation; they shared hopes, goals, and plans for the future, and they promised to be there for each other every step of the way. Soon they began to plan their wedding. Joe, his parents and siblings went formally to visit Uwa's parents and asked for her hand in marriage. Even though Uwa was not there, it turned out to be a beautiful ceremony.

Joe spoke of his goals and aspirations to marry Uwa while standing firm in front of her parents. There was a lot of love, laughter, and tears of happiness throughout their chat especially because they had known about their relationship for a long time and had met Joe several times before Uwa had departed to the United Kingdom.

The wedding date was finalised, and then the real planning started. There was a frenzy of activity and shared dreams as the expectation rose with each passing day. Uwa flew back home to wed Joe and finally, the day they had hoped for had come. A light breeze whispered the hope of a lovely day on this sunny morning. Anxieties and anticipation swirled in Uwa's chest as she faced a reflection in the mirror. The white-laced flowing bridal gown she wore looked beautiful on her and a veil of exquisite fabric framed her gorgeous face.

The town was in a state of heightened excitement as she approached the church. Many loved ones, some of whom had travelled long distances, gathered to celebrate Uwa and Joe's wedding. The majestic doors of the church swung open to unveil a stunning panorama. A string quartet played gentle music as a rainbow of flowers covered the aisle. Joe waited at the altar, breath held as he stared anxiously at the entrance. His grin and exquisitely designed tuxedo made him the centre of attention. He was taken aback by the sight of Uwa going down the aisle, a scene he had longed for. As soon as their gazes connected, the depth of their love for one another was special. As they exchanged self-written vows and wedding rings, surrounded by family and friends. There was a reception party following the church ceremony. The place was filled with people, food, drinks and music. Everyone was happy and danced the night away.

Following this, they agreed to put off their honeymoon until after Joe joined Uwa in the UK, and they put all of their energy into making that happen. Uwa soon flew back to the UK as she had to go back to her job. She had already completed her degree and was working as an administrative assistant in the marketing department of a highly esteemed organisation and she was earning a good wage.

About three months after their wedding, Joe joined Uwa in the UK and they started their forever journey together. Joe was happy with Uwa's choice of church and they attended together every Sunday. Joe started to learn how to drive and he soon got a job working in the post office as a clerk.

Most evenings, Uwa would make delicious meals which they ate together. They would then lie in each other's arms and Joe would listen to the news of the day while Uwa would read a novel. Over the next few months, Uwa began to feel sick with nausea and fever. She went to see her GP who confirmed she was pregnant. A few evenings after, Uwa found out that she was pregnant as the scent of their beloved Ogbono soup with pounded yam lingered in the air after they finished their dinner. Uwa finally broke her silence. Looking into Joe's eyes—those of her cherished husband—she felt her pulse race and her hands slightly perspire.

"Joe," she began, her voice trembling with a mix of excitement and uneasiness, "there's something I want to tell you."

Joe turned to face her, his eyes filled with interest. "What is it, love?" he asked, looking concerned

Uwa took a deep breath, her eyes shining with emotion. "I'm pregnant, Joe," she whispered, a radiant smile breaking across her face. There was a brief hush as Joe took in the words. His face then lit up with a broad, happy smile. Their hearts were racing with the immense joy that engulfed them as he drew Uwa closer and hugged her fiercely.

Uwa, oh my! Oh my goodness! Joe was surprised and elated at the same time as he shouted. He embraced her tightly, planting a gentle kiss on her forehead. "This is the best news, my love."

As they embraced one another, their hearts brimming with love and excitement, Uwa's eyes filled with tears. They had enjoyed innumerable joyful moments, but this one was special. The prospect of starting a family had only just started to alter their lives, bringing with it the type of happiness that could only be found at the start of a fresh chapter.

Though it appeared to be like a very long time, a few months later Uwa gave birth to a handsome baby boy and they named him Benjamin. Benjamin was such an adorable baby and Uwa and Joe enjoyed being parents for the first time. When Benjamin was five months old, Uwa became pregnant again, and Anne was born, bringing joy, love, and laughter into their family. As parents, Uwa and Joe were able to provide their children the same steadfast love and support that had united them, and they found themselves enjoying the experience.

Chapter 3 –
A Love Beyond Time

A few years after they tied the knot, tragedy struck. Joe became unwell and was diagnosed with cancer; the news brought sadness and worry to them. Uwa felt powerless as she witnessed her formerly dashing, robust, and devoted husband gradually deteriorate day by day. Joe and Uwa were so unhappy about this and over the next few months Joe's condition worsened. He spent a lot of time in and out of the hospital, which brought both joy and sadness into their lives. Every chance Uwa got, she spent in prayers. She would lift up her hands towards God and say, "Please, God, help me, heal Joe, I lift Joe up to You, Father, knowing that You are the ultimate healer." Uwa did not know what to do with herself. She feared for her future and that of her two children, Benjamin and Anne. Her emotions were all over the place. Some days she felt she had to be strong for Joe and other days she completely broke down and cried. She would sit by Joe's side in hospital holding his hand. She went with him for many tests, including blood tests, scans and meeting loads of specialists. Through it all, Uwa was there, providing continual comfort and reassurance, but the strain of caring for her husband Joe while he fought an unending sickness was unbearable. She was a young woman who had to care for her sick husband while also being far from her extended family. Caregiving became an even greater strain due to caring for Benjamin and Anne.

Uwa one day made a call to her parents in Nigeria and asked her mum to come and help her in the UK to assist with childcare for Benjamin and Anne, since Uwa was spending a lot of time in the hospital with Joe as his condition worsened, making it difficult for her to manage.

A week later, Uwa's mother arrived in the UK and immediately supported with the children, cooking, shopping and housekeeping. Uwa felt relieved and comforted. She would fall asleep each night with her mother holding her hand as they prayed together, offering her peace and encouraging her to trust on Jesus. Uwa and her mum would sing hymns and choruses that helped Uwa feel encouraged as she continued hoping in God that Joe would get better. Although Uwa's mum was a great help, there were other issues she needed to deal with such as the cost associated with commuting daily sometimes up to twice a day to and from the hospital, the emotional toll of seeing Joe in pain, and the moments of isolation she occasionally experienced. However, Uwa stuck by her husband through thick and thin and provided him the care he needed. She would sit long hours with him, even when he was drugged up and could not speak, stroking his hands and praying for him. She would attend to his personal care on a daily basis and would speak words of comfort and pray with Joe.

Uwa was a woman who possessed a wide range of skills, but her life was filled with the challenge of balancing her obligations as a devoted housewife and a mother who worked full-time. It was not uncommon for her days to be filled with a flurry of activity, which was frequently accompanied by the sound of her children laughing and the calming rhythm of housework. However, Uwa was also an agent for a cosmetic brand where she would sell both skin care and make up and she had developed a wide range of ladies who regularly purchased from her and introduced her to other ladies. Uwa loved to engage in conversation with her customers, who were women whom she had become friends with as a result of her enthusiasm and interest in their lives. Her "cosmetic meetings" took place on the two evenings that she had established for herself each week. During those evenings, Joe, who was known for his unwavering support, took it upon himself to take care of their children. The high-quality things that she sold and the specific attention that she showed to each transaction earned her a lot of admiration from her customers. For Uwa, selling cosmetics was not just about making a profit; it was about giving women the tools they needed to feel attractive and confident in themselves. She was aware that the purpose of cosmetics was not simply to hide imperfections; rather, it was to enhance all-natural beauty and to increase one's self-esteem. It was often the case that her house resembled a miniature beauty salon, as it included a large variety of products that were nicely organised and waiting to be shown. Whenever Uwa's customers showed up for their scheduled appointments, they were greeted with a friendly grin and a real interest in the beauty requirements they had. Uwa provided individualised advice and direction during each session, which turned into an occasion for connection and bonding between the two of them. However, due to Joe's ill health, Uwa had to put a temporary stop to selling cosmetics. She battled with this decision, to either see Joe on those evenings or to sell her cosmetics and the reason being that this time it was because she needed the money. There was hardly any revenue from Joe's employers, as he had been sick for too long and his sick pay had ended. Uwa was even considering signing Joe up to get benefits but she knew he hated that a lot. She prayed to God and asked for his wisdom in making the right decision for her family and for strength to go through these difficult days.

Uwa also had another issue, one where she found herself advocating for Joe and ensuring that he had the highest possible level of care. At a certain point in time, there were instances of optimism, such as when Joe displayed indications of progress, and Uwa would permit herself to fantasise about a more favourable future. However, these times were frequently followed by setbacks, which were extremely distressing for both of them. Uwa maintained her steadfastness in God.

Joe's health continued to deteriorate over time, despite the fact that they made every attempt to save him and that he received medical attention. As the condition of her cherished spouse continued to deteriorate, Uwa stared helplessly. And then, in a moment that rocked her entire universe, he passed away. The day Joe passed away it was like time stood still for Uwa. She instantly lost her memory, her confidence, her zeal to life and she felt exposed to the world.

Having to deal with the arrangements for the funeral of her cherished husband, Joe, was an extremely exhausting and difficult event. In order to pay tribute to Joe's memory and commemorate his life, it was necessary to make a number of decisions, solicit assistance from those who were dear to him, handle the financial issues, and strike a balance between maintaining traditions and adding personal touches. Uwa and the children were able to say their final goodbyes and share memories of Joe during the funeral, which marked the beginning of the mourning process. Uwa was aware that she needed to be strong, particularly for Benjamin and Anne, due to the fact that they were still so young. She frequently questioned whether or not they were aware that their father had passed away. Uwa would frequently respond to Anne's enquiries by saying, "Dad is now in heaven as an angel while he watches over us." Each and every weekend, the three of them would spend a significant amount of time looking at family photographs. Benjamin suddenly became a big boy and always hugged Uwa.

In light of Joe's passing, the years of love, the dreams they had in common, and the lovely moments they had built together now felt like a bittersweet experience together. Uwa's heart was heavy with sorrow, but she continued to draw strength from the memories they had shared together and the lessons they had learnt together after some time had passed. Uwa's heart and the children that they had brought into the world were the places where Joe's legacy continued to live on. She came to the conclusion that she would commemorate his legacy by infusing his principles, love, and spirit in the rearing of their children.

Within few weeks of Joe's passing, widowhood started to present its difficulties to Uwa. In her prayers to God, she would express her sorrow, grief, and questions, seeking comfort and strength. She found solace in prayer and found strength in reading texts to help her overcome her weaknesses. Uwa held tight onto scriptures such as Isaiah 41:10 (NLT)—"Don't be afraid, for I am with you—"—was one of her favourite. Keep going because I am your God. You may count on my support and strength. With my triumphant right hand, I shall support you.

Uwa had a good community and support network around her including her family, friends, church members, and devoted customers. The support she received from them gave her the strength to go on, even in the face of her loss. But before long, Uwa's mum had to go back to Nigeria, leaving her with the kids and a handful of friends who dropped by every now and then to see how they were doing.

Over time, Uwa adapted to a new role—one she had never anticipated taking on. From the beginning, people referred to her as "the widow" or "the lady whose husband recently passed away". The burden of her loss and the new anguish it had brought was heavy on these titles. But then, as time passed, a lovely thing started to happen. Her image as an energetic, passionate lady began to change over time in the eyes of the people. Word spread about "the lady whose husband passed away a few years ago", and as time went on, the memories of her resiliency and fortitude supplanted the grief that had previously defined her. It's like, "You know, the one who sells cosmetics."

After Joe passed away, Uwa embarked on a trip that gave her strength and direction. She became an inspiration to others, especially widows, by transforming her sorrow into something lovely and meaningful. Uwa began sharing her story of perseverance and providing advice and comfort to other women who had also gone through loss at women's conferences.

Uwa continued to be steadfast in her dedication to her cosmetics business, but she also took a daring leap forward. In order to have a more direct relationship with her clientele, she decided to create a store. She expanded her cosmetics and included a hairstyling service in her new shop. Uwa found that this embanked her to make extra money and also allowed her be there to care for Benjamin and Anne. This eased the financial burden of looking after a family that had once had two incomes. A long-standing aspect of Uwa's identity was her skill as a creator of traditional Nigerian hairstyles. She named her shop "Hair and Faces" and she focused on providing excellent customer care.

Uwa's unwavering determination and the success of her business served as an inspiration to her and everyone around her. She was able to provide her children the best possible care and an atmosphere they could grow up in since her beauty parlour and hairstyling business took off. Working at the shop gave her kids a chance to see the significance of following one's dreams and the benefits of perseverance. Uwa had always wanted to move from working as a career woman to owning her own business. The children learnt about Uwa's cultural traditions and the business world in a one-of-a-kind setting that was both educational and enjoyable.

Uwa counted it as an immense blessing that Aunty B's influence was still strong in her life. She was an integral part of their support system, more than just an aunt; she was a kind and supportive figure. Uwa and her children would frequently get hearty Nigerian meals prepared by Aunty B, who was very generous with her time and energy. This gesture of generosity represented more than just giving food; it was an expression of caring and love.

In Uwa's healing process and life in general, her faith group and her circle of friends were crucial. Even in the midst of her struggles, she found comfort and strength in the community of her church, where she received spiritual counsel, prayers, and a feeling of belonging. These reliable friends became a rock of constant encouragement and company. Uwa knew she could trust them, rely on them, and seek their counsel, solace, and comprehension when she needed it.

Chapter 4 – A Friend In Need is a Bloody Nuisance

One such close friend was Nkechi, who had been by Uwa's side since the day she'd heard the devastating news. Nkechi's home had become a sanctuary for Uwa during those dark days. Uwa and her kids would most evenings go from Uwa's shop to Nkechi's house, where they would have dinner and spend the evening.

Most times while Nkechi made the evening meal, Uwa would support her children and Nkechi's children in doing their homework. Other times she would help Nkechi in the kitchen, especially to wash up after dinner. She would always call her daughter Anne to join her in tidying the kitchen before they left for home. In addition, Uwa made sure she always brought some groceries now and again when she came to visit Nkechi and her family in consideration to the fact that she and her two kids ate in Nkechi's house on a regular basis.

Uwa felt happy this way and was very grateful for the support her friend Nkechi was giving her. Some evenings, Uwa would find solace in Nkechi's company. They would sit on the porch, sipping tea, sharing stories, and comforting each other through the emotional turbulence. Uwa felt blessed to have a friend like Nkechi, who offered unwavering support during her most challenging moments.

Nkechi's life was a tapestry weaved with love, culture, and the complexity of relationships. Her experience as a beautiful, fair-skinned woman from Nigeria's Igbo region married to a Yoruba man was filled with both joy and challenges. The main source of her distress was her strained relationship with her mother-in-law. Nkechi experienced a separation between herself and her mother-in-law from the start. She couldn't help but suspect that her mother-in-law didn't think highly of her, and her mother-in-law's aloof demeanour further confirmed this suspicion. Her mother-in-law's refusal to answer Nkechi's calls or contact with her children exacerbated their growing rift. Nkechi's bad connection with her mother-in-law became a recurring source of conflict in her marriage. It frequently resulted in furious disputes between Nkechi and her husband, who found himself torn between his allegiance to his wife and his mum.

Nkechi and Uwa had a deep and supportive friendship that allowed them to confide in each other about their individual struggles. Their chats frequently focused on the difficulties of their lives, allowing them to express their frustrations, share their dreams, and provide mutual comfort and understanding. Weeks passed into months, and their daily nighttime encounters became a familiar pattern.

A few months later, Uwa began to notice a subtle alteration in Nkechi's attitude. Nkechi's demeanour had deteriorated, and their encounters had grown more strained. Uwa was perplexed and concerned by Nkechi's behaviour change. She wondered whether something had happened in Nkechi's life that was prompting her to withdraw from their friendship. Uwa, being the sensitive and compassionate friend she was, wanted to have an open and honest chat with Nkechi to determine what was bothering her. "Nkechi," Uwa began, picking a time when they could converse alone, "I've observed that things have been a little different between us lately. Is anything on your mind? Have I done anything to upset you?"

Nkechi paused for a time, her face a mixture of emotions. She then confided in Uwa about her own personal issues and struggles. She said that the stress and complications in her life had caused her to retreat from several of her social relationships, including their friendship. Aside from that, Nkechi said nothing and remained unfriendly.

One cool bright summer evening, Uwa's steps were unsure as she approached Nkechi's house with Benjamin and Anne behind her. She couldn't avoid the idea that she was visiting too frequently, and her presence was becoming bothersome. However, when they discussed this, Nkechi made no clear indication of requesting less interaction. Uwa fought with her thoughts as she approached Nkechi's door. She was torn between wanting to be there for her friend and worrying about overstepping limits. As she stood there, the choice weighing on her, she decided to follow her instincts and be honest with Nkechi.

When Nkechi answered the door and saw Uwa, she gave her a kind but puzzled grin. After exchanging greetings, Uwa gently brought up the matter that had been upsetting her. "Nkechi," Uwa said, her voice tinged with concern, "I've been coming over pretty frequently, and I'm beginning to wonder if it's becoming too much for you. I don't want to take up your space or make you uncomfortable."

Uwa had not anticipated what Nkechi would say next. "Uwa, we need to talk," Nkechi said, her voice shaking with hesitation. Uwa, bewildered and apprehensive, sat down, and she realised something was wrong. Nkechi took a big breath and stated, "Uwa, I want you to know how much I care about you and how supportive I have been during this difficult time. But lately, it's becoming difficult for me. I have a family and duties, and it seems like you're around virtually every evening. I don't mean to be harsh, but I need some space."

Uwa was taken aback, and her eyes filled with tears. "Nkechi, I never meant to burden you. You've been my rock throughout this difficult time, and I'm very grateful for your help. Since Joe died seven months ago," Uwa continued, "I have come to depend on you and that has been insensitive of me. I understand your desire for space and will respect it." Then it occurred to Uwa that Nkechi might be joking, as in the last two months she had stopped visiting every day as she had when Joe first died; she now only came a few times a week, and she always made sure to give back to Nkechi as much as Nkechi provided to her.

Uwa enquired, "Nkechi, are you joking? You should have said this a long time ago instead of getting distant and making me feel welcome when that was no longer the case. You should have been honest; I assumed our friendship had progressed to the point where we could always be honest with one another."

Nkechi interrupted her. "Well, I am not joking; Joe is not coming back and I think you and your kids should move on " She continued to claim that she valued and cherished their friendship, but it was putting a strain on her. That was when Uwa realised her friend wasn't joking. Nkechi's comments and tone were sincere and honest, leaving no question. Uwa's initial mistrust gave way to genuine gratitude for the understanding and support she was receiving. It became evident that Nkechi's intentions were genuine, and Uwa felt deeply grateful for their relationship and mutual understanding.

Uwa praised Nkechi and apologised for not being more sensitive to her friend's sentiments earlier. She revealed to Nkechi that it had crossed her mind once or twice, but she'd reduced her daily visits to a few times a week, unaware that even that was too much for Nkechi. Uwa replied with, "Nkechi, my dear sister, I have become so used to coming to you and that is selfish of me, knowing you have your own issues." Nkechi exhaled, appearing relieved that she had been able to express her thoughts to Uwa. Uwa went on to say, "After all, a friend in need is a friend indeed, and I really appreciate all of your support for my kids and me, Nkechi," but Nkechi responded with a hash and a higher tone of voice. "No, Uwa, a friend in need is a bloody nuisance." As Nkechi stated those words, she rose up and turned to face the television, maybe to avoid looking her friend in the eyes or to change the channel.

Uwa was taken aback by these harsh words and thanked Nkechi once more for all of her help. Uwa summoned her two children, who were already playing happily, to collect their belongings. Sensing their mother's desperation, the children rushed to pack their belongings, and they were ready to leave Nkechi's house in a matter of minutes. They all said their goodbyes, and Uwa and her children proceeded to their car. Uwa burst into tears as soon as she got inside her car. Benjamin and Anne hugged her, held her hands, and prayed with her. "Dear God, please help our mummy; she is going through a lot." They continued to cuddle and soothe her, despite the fact that they were children and had no idea what had caused their mother's tears.

Uwa dried her eyes and blew her nose with a tissue before looking into her children's eyes, which were filled with pride and devotion, and said, "You are both so amazing, and I love you more than words can express. Thank you for being such lovely children." Uwa kissed each of their foreheads and remarked cheerfully, "Let us go home and to bed; tomorrow will be a better day." Her children smiled and embraced their mother, returning her devotion with sweet, innocent hugs. They drove home silently.

Uwa kept thinking about Nkechi's remarks, "A friend in need is a bloody nuisance," and felt hurt and deceived by them. It implied that Uwa's presence and need for assistance were perceived as annoying and troublesome, which was a stark contrast to the care and comfort she had come to expect from her buddy. Uwa's anguish made her feel even more alone and abandoned. She knew she needed to move on, and she had been coming to Nkechi's place for far too long, and she should have known better. Uwa felt disappointed in herself for not being wise enough to halt and discover alternative ways to deal with her situation.

Uwa learnt a terrible lesson that day, one that would stick with her for years. It was a lesson in the nature of human support, the limits of friendship, and the importance of faith in her life.

As she reflected on Nkechi's harsh words, Uwa realised that everyone, no matter how close or caring, had limitations. Nkechi's statements served as a clear reminder that individuals may become exhausted, overwhelmed, and face their own challenges. Uwa had erroneously placed unrealistic expectations on her friend, anticipating unwavering support in her time of need. This realisation led Uwa to deepen her faith. She recognised that only God could supply unwavering support. Her faith became her anchor, a source of strength and comfort when human support failed. Uwa also came to recognise the value of self-reliance. While friends and family were vital sources of support, she recognised the importance of developing inner strength and resilience in order to face life's obstacles. Relying solely on others for assistance may be emotionally demanding for both parties.

Uwa also learned to accept the imperfections of people, including herself. Nkechi's hurtful statement, though painful, was a reminder that humans were flawed and sometimes said or did things out of their own limitations and emotions. Uwa found it within herself to forgive and accept these imperfections, recognizing that true friendship involved understanding and compassion. In the end, Uwa's hard lesson transformed her perspective on life and friendship. She now understood the delicate balance between human support and personal strength, and the central role her faith played in providing unwavering comfort during trying times. This lesson, though learned through pain, would serve as a source of wisdom and personal growth for Uwa in the years to come.

The hurtful statement, "A friend in need is a bloody nuisance," uttered by Nkechi, significantly strained Uwa's and Nkechi's friendship and ultimately caused a deep rift between them. Uwa felt emotionally wounded and rejected by Nkechi's insensitive words. It left her feeling unsupported and unappreciated during a time when she was vulnerable and grieving the loss of her husband. This wound festered, creating an emotional barrier between them.

Resentment began to build within Uwa as she pondered Nkechi's lack of empathy and support. She felt that the person she had considered her closest friend had let her down during a time when she needed her the most. The resentment eroded the trust and closeness that had previously characterized their friendship. In response to the hurtful statement, Uwa started distancing herself emotionally from Nkechi, fearing further rejection or inconvenience. This emotional withdrawal created a gap between them, making it difficult for them to connect as they once did. Although they attended the same church and would see each other most Sundays and during other church programmes, Uwa preferred to keep her distance from Nkechi. She would make sure she did not sit near her or park her car near hers in order to completely avoid her.

Eventually, the divide between Uwa and Nkechi resulted in a drift between them. Despite their once-close bond, they were unable to bridge the emotional gap, and their friendship began to wither, leaving them feeling distant and disconnected from one another. Uwa moved away from that area and changed church and she never saw Nkechi ever again. The incident with Nkechi had a lasting impact on Uwa. She carried the memory of that hurtful statement with her throughout the years. It shaped how she approached and formed new friendships. Uwa became more cautious, taking the lessons learned from her experience with Nkechi and applying them to her interactions with others.

She was keen to establish boundaries and communicate openly with her new friends, understanding that friendships needed nurturing, empathy, and respect for each other's needs and boundaries. The painful experience with Nkechi had made her more discerning in choosing friends who would be supportive and understanding, and she valued the lessons learned from her past friendship as she moved forward in life. Once again, Uwa had lost a solid friendship as she and Nkechi never crossed paths again.

Uwa's life had taken another heart-wrenching turn, and she found herself navigating the difficult path of grief once more. The loss of her husband, her close friends, and the security of her familiar church community left her feeling adrift in a sea of uncertainty. She decided to move completely to a new area. The struggles and challenges of looking for a new home for her and the kids, looking for a new school for the kids, looking for a new job for herself as she had closed her shop and looking for a new church was all overwhelming, but she held on to her faith and knew that God would see her through like he always did. Though her heart ached with sorrow, Uwa also found resilience within herself. She recalled the strength she had drawn from her past experiences, the love she had shared with her late husband, and the friendships that had once filled her life with joy. These memories became a wellspring of courage, propelling her to face the new challenges that lay ahead.

Chapter 5 –
A Lying Tongue

There were a lot of things that happened to Uwa that she felt would have been different or less impactful had Joe been alive. But she chose to move on. Soon she found a smaller apartment compared to where she and the children had lived with Joe when he was alive. Uwa also found a new church in her new neighbourhood and began attending, but she started to feel and notice the critical looks and hushed conversations from a few members of the congregation every time she entered the church.

Many people treated her differently because she was a widow and a single mother. Somehow, she felt that the congregation was excluding her because of the invisible scarlet letter on her status. It seemed like her fellow churchgoers shunned her due to her sorrow and her situation. Uwa yearned to be a part of the church community, to enjoy sharing her faith with others and to take part in all the events and activities that the church had to offer.

She had thought so many times of leaving and looking for another local church, but Benjamin and Anne liked the children's session of the church, and they had a very good Sunday school teacher. They seemed to be learning more about the bible and how to pray better from the children church evident in their family prayer and bible study at home. For this reason, Uwa decided to stay and bear the snubs. On one Sunday service, one of the men in the church chose to belittle her and accuse her of a terrible deed. This man approached her while she was busy with her own affairs, being condescending and judgemental the whole time, insinuating that she was attempting to attract male attention in the church with her fair complexion which he said he was so sure it was not natural but she was bleaching her skin. The claim was hurtful and unfounded because it attacked Uwa's character and integrity. The accusation pierced her heart like a blade. Already, she had to deal with the difficulties of being a single mother on top of the shame associated with being a widow, the loss of her husband, her community, and her church. It was demoralising and emotionally traumatic to have a fellow churchgoer disrespect her in this way. Uwa was appalled that a member of her religious group would make such a baseless and damaging accusation, especially because she had never participated in such acts. Her faith in the Christian community crumbled, and she felt ashamed and alone. Uwa battled to keep her cool and suppressed her emotions as she faced this unjustified assault on her persona. It brought back the hurtful memories of the cruel treatment she had endured since becoming a church member and exacerbated the stigma and isolation she had been suffering. She walked off with her children and made her way to her car without uttering her precious breath to address this vile man. What was more hurtful was that the pastor or any of the leaders of the church did not correct this evil act.

 The day Uwa endured the cruel accusations and insults at the church was a watershed moment in her life. The mental and emotional strain had become intolerable, so she made the tough decision to quit going to that church completely. She knew she needed to make a change for her own mental health because the place she had sought refuge had turned out to be a refuge of loneliness and misery. Uwa did not take her decision to depart from the church lightly. Even more discouraging, though, was the Christian community's apparent indifference. Nobody contacted her to find out why she'd vanished so suddenly. She seemed to have vanished into thin air, as if her mere existence had been insignificant to them, rendering her departure insignificant. Silence from other worshippers brought up terrible memories of how alone she had felt at that church.

Uwa started staying at home on Sundays. She and the kids would sing and dance to worship songs and share some bible stories. However, after realising that she and the kids had been spiritually suffering from staying home on Sundays for nearly a month, Uwa decided to search for a new church to attend. After some research, she located one that she thought her family would enjoy. Compared to her last encounter, the new church she discovered was very different. Everyone felt welcome, and the members went out of their way to help one another. The fact that Uwa was a widow and a single mother no longer made her an outcast. She was welcomed with open arms and accepted as an esteemed member of the community. She found a home there and was content; the kids also made friends and loved going to church. She devoted her life to serving the Lord and joined the ushering department. Additionally, Uwa had started a new job and she progressed quickly to a higher grade as project manager, and with this she was able to achieve all of her professional and financial commitments while still advancing her career. Project and team management were areas in which she thrived in her position, which gave her ample opportunity to put her abilities to use. After all she had been through, it was a breath of fresh air, and she felt stronger and more capable as a result. Uwa also started to take use of the training opportunities in her work organisation to take short courses that helped her climb the corporate ladder.

Friendships and connections of significance began to take shape as Uwa immersed herself further in her new church and community. She became friends with other moms at her children's school. Her friends and acquaintances eventually took note of her resiliency and the courage with which she had triumphed over adversity, particularly the death of her husband. It came to pass that

Uwa was being pushed to think about dating again by her friends and her newfound support system. Their sincere want was for her to find the happiness and satisfaction that a new love relationship may have offered. Like most of her friends said... it had been three years since Joe had passed away. Uwa, although initially hesitant, began to entertain the idea of dating again. She recognized that her friends and the community around her had her best interests at heart and that their encouragement came from a place of caring and support. The thought of a new chapter in her life, one that might include love and companionship, stirred a sense of hope within her.

The courageous decision to sign up for a Christian dating service by Uwa was an exploration of the prospect of rediscovering love and companionship. She had high hopes that this platform may introduce her to Christian men who were sincere, open, and seeking true relationships. Unfortunately, she had a negative and irritating experience on the dating service. Uwa met men who let her down by not being as honest and forthright as she had wished. Her hopes were dashed because so many of them had lied to her. Uwa discovered that there were many people in the world who were dishonest and whose words never matched their actions.

One faithful day, Uwa received an unusual call from an unknown number; a man's voice greeted her with "Hi," after Uwa asked, "Who is speaking, please?" The man introduced himself as "Abbey" and reiterated his need to meet with Boye.

"You have a wrong number because there is no Boye here," Uwa remarked.

After Abbey continued by explaining that he'd run into an old school mate and he'd asked if the person knew Boye's number as he and Boye were roommates in university, and he was given this number, he apologised and ended the call. A few minutes later, another call came in, same voice, same man and same conversation. Uwa once again said she did not know anyone by the name of Boye. The caller claimed that he'd called again as perhaps he had entered the wrong numbers earlier, so he tried calling again. Abbey then spoke with Uwa for a few minutes, mostly exchanging pleasantries, before he once again apologised and ended the call. Two days after their brief phone talk, Uwa was surprised to receive a call from Abbey; he said that he'd called because he had been thinking about her since they'd first spoken. Abbey said Uwa had a calming voice that piqued his interest, and he wanted to know her more. Uwa was wary at first because of her experiences with dishonest people, but she was captivated by Abbey's words. He appeared different from men she had met recently; his voice was calm and he appeared authentic. That day formed the beginning of many nights of conversations as Uwa and Abbey began to get to know one another. Uwa liked that he was forthright about how he felt and how much he wanted to know her.

She was informed by Abbey that he was a 44-year-old social worker who worked for the local council in the area he resided in. He spoke highly of himself as an empathetic and hard-working professional who cherished his work and had a strong calling to aid those in need. People dealing with poverty, family problems, and mental health issues were among the many societal challenges he helped alleviate in his work. Abbey maintained a healthy work-life balance despite the demands of his position. Abbey told Uwa about his past relationships. He had been through the highs and lows of marriage and had a son from a prior relationship; he was now divorced. He appeared to be an attentive and kind father who did his best to set a good example and provide for his son in the best way he could. Abbey also told Uwa about his last girlfriend and said the relationship did not work out due to differences they both had and could not reconcile.

Uwa came to the conclusion that Abbey was a decent man based on this and their other conversations. Not only was he a Christian, which made Uwa very happy, but he also seemed to care about her. Their bond became stronger as Uwa and Abbey persisted in spending hours each night conversing over the phone. Deep into their own histories, aspirations, and personal tales, their interactions transcended the superficial. As their bond deepened, Uwa found solace in opening up to Abbey about the pain of her past and her recollections of Joe.

Uwa and Abbey decided to meet face-to-face to formalise their burgeoning romance as they had only been communicating through chats and calls. Uwa invited Abbey to spend the weekend at her house after they discussed their intentions. Because it would put them in an atmosphere where they could relax and get to know one another better, it was a big deal for them both. To Uwa they were both adults and this seemed like the next progression in their relationship. At the said weekend, Uwa took the kids to Aunty B's house for the weekend straight from school so she had enough time to prepare dinner for Abbey. Uwa told Aunty B about her new love and as usual Aunty was very happy with this news, saying, "It is time you found love again." Uwa preferred a quiet, one-on-one setting for their first face-to-face meeting, away from the distractions of her children, so that they could concentrate on getting to know one another. She wanted to make sure that any introduction between Abbey and her children would be done properly and at the right time, which represented her protective instincts as a single mother.

Before Abbey's long-awaited arrival on Friday night, Uwa made sure everything was in order. She cooked up a storm for Abbey's supper, which included fried chicken, fried rice, gizzards and dodo, salad, and fish pepper soup. After Uwa finished preparing the food, she made sure the house was clean, and then she went to take a shower. She put on a pleasant fragrance and chose to wear a simple dress that she had purchased from her favourite internet retailer. Perfumes were Uwa's favourite and she loved to mix two to three together, which she did. Uwa wore her make up too. Jewels that sparkled in her eyes completed her outfit. As she was rounding off her dressing, Uwa received a text message from Abbey stating that he would be at the train station nearest to her house in about ten to fifteen minutes. Abbey mentioned that he'd opted to take the train instead of driving to avoid heavy Friday traffic. Abbey lived approximately one hour and thirty minutes away from Uwa by train. The station was only a short three-minute drive from Uwa's house, so she was thrilled to tell him she would pick him up. On her way to collect him, Uwa could feel her enthusiasm growing. The person she had formed such a strong bond with over the phone was finally coming to visit, and she was looking forward to spending meaningful time with him.

When Uwa and Abbey finally met in person, they held one another in a loving embrace, and a smile spread across their cheeks. It was an authentic moment of bonding that mirrored the chemistry they had been developing during their phone calls and chats. As Uwa embraced Abbey, a surge of longing and want surged through her. She hadn't felt such a deep connection or the longing to be held by a guy in a very long time. She had guarded her heart since Joe's death, but being in Abbey's company was causing her defences to fall down. There was more at play here than mere sexual desire; there was also the hope for a fresh start and the profound emotional bond they had formed.

The night was filled with joy and laughter, and Uwa felt happy and peaceful. They went to bed very late talking and embracing one another. On Saturday morning, they awoke in each other's embrace, and they were met with a feeling of pure contentment and genuine ease with one another. The room was bathed in a soft light as the morning sun poured through the windows. They spent the Saturday in conversation, playing games of Monopoly and Ludo and watching a movie. What surprised Uwa was how hands-on and domestic Abbey was, He helped her do some housework and ironed the kids' school uniforms. He also helped her do some manly jobs that she had needed in the house including changing a bulb, hanging the curtain in the kitchen that was falling off and fixing a broken dining table chair. As they were both church workers and the next day was a Sunday, they agreed Abbey would return to his home with the last train on Saturday night. Uwa dropped Abbey at the station and he said goodbye, and they were already missing each other. Abbey assured Uwa that he would give her a call the moment he got home.

It was reasonable for Uwa to feel worried and anxious as the evening progressed without hearing from Abbey. There was no answer or connection when she called him over twenty times. Concerned about what might have transpired, she was genuinely disturbed by the lack of response from him. Uwa didn't get much sleep that night. Early the next morning, Uwa got ready for church and decided to pick Benjamin and Anne from her aunt's place so they went to church together. On her way, she tried calling Abbey again but got disconnected each time. On arrival at Aunty B's house, the kids were ready and were excited to see her. Aunty B was also on her way to church so the timing was perfect. The kids got into the car and started to tell their mum about the lovely time they'd had in Aunty B's house; as usual, they'd been well taken care of and spoilt. This discussion, and since she had been missed her children terribly, offered a comfort to her heart. Church was nice and she prayed for Abbey's safety. Over the next few days, Uwa was sad since Abbey never responded. She decided to call the local council where Abbey told her he worked, and she was informed that no such person was employed there, so she proceeded to contact the church where he had stated he attended and was also informed that no such person was a member. She had once again faced a lying tongue. Uwa had no choice but to continue with her life as usual, devoting herself to her career, the children, and her church duties. Additionally, she made the decision to resume some of the charitable work she had previously done, specifically with young women, particularly widows.

About a year after the incident with Abbey, Uwa got a call from Rob, an old friend of Joe, who had called her to see how she and the kids were doing. Rob used to call a lot after Joe died but that faded and Uwa understood as she knew everyone was busy and they all needed to get on with their lives, but then he abruptly stopped doing so. Rob apologised that he had not been calling and said he was coming to visit her and the kids over the weekend. Rob did not drive but also did not live far away from Uwa and the kids. True to his words, Rob visited on Saturday, and the kids were delighted to see him. They all went to the park and went to eat lunch, and afterwards Uwa dropped Rob at home. It was a lovely day especially as there were loads of talks about Joe, and the kids enjoyed Uncle Rob telling them tales about their dad from their youth days. The next day, Uwa called Rob to thank him and Rob told her that he had left his jacket in the trunk of her car. Uwa said she was happy to drop it off for him the next evening. Uwa kept her promise and arrived at Rob's shared apartment. She knocked on the main door and it was opened by a man whom she assumed to be Rob's flat mate. She told him she was looking for Rob and he said, "Welcome, come right in and go straight up the stairs, you will find Rob there," he replied, his voice and face looking so familiar. Uwa was trying to think of if and how she knew this man. She wondered why he appeared so familiar to her as she climbed the stairs looking for Rob.

On getting up the stairs, Uwa called out, "Rob, it's Uwa," and he came out of his room, welcoming Uwa.

Uwa said, "Here is your jacket."

Rob replied, "Thanks, how was your day and how are the kids?"

Uwa, "They are fine and currently at lesson."

Uwa then asked Rob, "Who is that man downstairs?" and Rob said, "Oh, that is Biodun, my flat mate."

Uwa replied, "He looks so familiar," and suddenly her memory came to light and she remembered how she knew him. That was Abbey. She asked again so his name is Biodun and Rob said yes. Uwa was so sure and shocked, and said in her mind, "Wow, this is the lying tongue." She said to Rob, "Please excuse me, I think I know him, and I want to ask him if he is the person I think he is."

Uwa proceeded to go down the stairs and knocked on the door she had seen the man go into after he let her in the house. With a mix of emotions, including relief, worry, and curiosity, Uwa simply said, "Abbey" when he opened the door. Her utterance of his name conveyed her immediate need for answers and her desire to understand why he had gone silent, leaving her in a state of anxiety. Uwa's surprise and confusion deepened when the man at the door denied being Abbey. It was a disheartening and perplexing moment for her, as she had been so certain it was him. However, Uwa was not willing to let this situation go unquestioned. Fuelled by a mix of frustration and determination, she confronted the man and firmly expressed her belief, saying, "I am not dumb; I know you are Abbey. I cannot forget the one I spent a beautiful night with."

Suddenly, Abbey held his head over his hands and said, "Uwa I am so ashamed of myself, I cannot even look you in the eye, Uwa. I am so sorry."

Uwa said, "I am confused. So you live local to me? So you know Rob? So what happened?" She had a million questions running through her head and mouth at the same time. Abbey knelt down in front of Uwa and began to beg her for forgiveness, acknowledging his initial denial and expressing a willingness to explain. He said he did not want Rob to hear what they were discussing. By this time, Uwa was shouting at him and calling him all sorts of names. Rob rushed in asking what the matter was.

    Abbey's face sank as soon as he saw Rob. He acknowledged that he had done something wrong and expressed his regret for it. Abbey went on to explain that Rob had frequently spoken about Uwa and how much he admired her. He revealed that Rob had wanted to date her because he found her to be a kind and wonderful person. However, he felt he could not do so because Uwa's late husband had been a close friend of his when he was alive from their days as youths back home in Nigeria and they each knew each other's families. Abbey said the more Rob spoke of Uwa, the more he wanted to meet her and one day when Rob was having a shower, he took Rob's phone and got Uwa's number from it without Rob's knowledge. Uwa found that hard to believe and all that could come to her mouth was, "What a lying tongue you are." Abbey continued and said it was after that he called Uwa and pretended to be calling to speak to someone and proceeded to lie to her, visit her. He said he was not a social worker and all he did and said were lies but that he genuinely liked Uwa. By this time she was boiling with rage. Abbey said his full name was Abiodun which could be shortened to Abbey or Biodun. He said that was the only thing he did not lie about but that everything else he said about his job, where he lived, were all lies. Abbey said after he left Uwa that Saturday pretending to be going back to home that he knew he could not continue the relationship as there was no way he could explain himself to Rob or get away with the lies, hence he decided it was best to just cut Uwa off immediately. He never knew their paths would ever cross again. Uwa replied, "How dumb are you? You live in the same house with Rob and you never felt our paths would cross again?" Rob's anger and Uwa's tears were understandable reactions to the situation. Rob had every reason to be upset, as his trust had been breached and his privacy violated when his phone number was taken without his consent. Uwa, on the other hand, was overwhelmed with hurt and bitterness, feeling betrayed and used. For Uwa, this situation felt like yet another instance of trust being broken, adding to her history of difficult experiences and disappointments. Her emotions, including anger and sadness, reflected the deep sense of violation and hurt that she was feeling.

In the wake of the revelations and the complex emotions that had arisen, Uwa made the difficult decision to remove herself from the situation. She wasn't sure if Abbey had been entirely honest, and there was lingering doubt about whether Rob had willingly given him her number. The trust had been significantly eroded, and Uwa felt a profound sense of hurt and confusion. Her choice to step away from both Abbey and Rob was driven by the need to protect herself and take time to process her emotions and thoughts. Facing the pain, confusion, and disappointment she had experienced, Uwa turned to her faith and sought solace in her relationship with God.

In prayer and reflection, Uwa found a pathway to healing, forgiveness, and understanding. She sought peace in her heart and the wisdom to navigate the complexities of her relationships with Abbey and Rob. Uwa's faith was an integral part of her journey to overcome adversity and find a sense of closure and hope for the future. She overcame the lying tongue.

She held on to this scripture from the bible –
Philippians 4:6-7 (NLT)

"Don't worry about anything; instead, pray about everything. Tell God what you need and thank him for all he has done. Then you will experience God's peace, which exceeds anything we can understand. His peace will guard your hearts and minds as you live in Christ Jesus."

Uwa took time to reflect on this experience, especially for her to understand more the part she'd played and what she could have done better, or better still, what she would do differently next time. Uwa agreed to never let a man in her house again until she was so sure about him. She would be wined and dined in public before she took him seriously, and she would check out the information given as well. Uwa being the strong and resilient woman she was said, "I can never be fooled again, God helping me."

Chapter 6 –
And She Said YES

Uwa found herself in challenging situations on numerous occasions, and she was always miserable, and her GP eventually diagnosed her with depression and anxiety. He also started her on some anti-depressants. Uwa had never really been one that liked medication as she felt every medication solved one issue but might have a side effect and bring up another issue. She had always used her faith to elevate her mood and it worked, but now she had come to realise the place that medication would play in helping her recover and stay strong for herself and her children. The decision to take the medication was also due to Uwa's inability to sleep at night. She was having terrible difficulty with sleep, and insomnia now became a regular part of her life. It was so bad that Uwa actually expected not to sleep whenever she went to bed. She believed she had faced her fair share of trials in life. Adversity seemed to find her, and she frequently found herself asking a question in her quiet moments of prayer: "Why do I have so many challenges?" Her faith continued to provide the much-needed solace, and she would always go to the place of prayer, a place where she could pour out her heart and seek comfort in God, her maker. Though the solutions to her questions did not come in the form of words, Uwa's faith was a constant companion. It gave her the strength to persevere, even when the weight of her challenges seemed terrible.

Uwa was sanguine; this was her personality and she knew and carried it well. Always bubbly, cheerful and happy. This resulted in so many close friends not actually knowing she was depressed and had insomnia. Uwa too found it hard to ask for help especially after her experience years ago with Nkechi.

Uwa used her resilience and strength she had found in God to make some adjustments in her life after seeing the value of accepting new possibilities and experiences. With renewed motivation, she began to socialise more and decided to also look for a better job. She soon found work in the buzzing city of London. This change gave her the opportunity to broaden her horizons and experience the dynamic urban environment. While she welcomed this new professional chapter, Uwa continued to enjoy living in the serene suburbs, striking a balance between the activity of the city and the tranquillity of suburban life. This was important to her as she also had to consider her wonderful children in all she did.

Uwa's children had grown into teenagers, and their lives were beginning to take shape in unique ways. They had their own interests, friends, and activities that kept them occupied and engaged outside of the home. Uwa observed with pleasure and nostalgia as her children travelled the world, made friends, and built their own identities. The once-busy household had become calmer, and Uwa had more time for herself. Her work took up her time, with her ministry and hobbies not left out.

Uwa decided to socialise after work one Friday evening with her colleagues who had invited her to a local pub for a drink. It was a rare moment of calm and a chance to decompress after her hectic day. As she sipped her drink and enjoyed the atmosphere at the pub, she struck up a discussion with a kind stranger. He introduced himself to her as Solomon. They became immersed in discussion, telling stories and getting to know each other, and within a few hours it felt like they had known each other for years. Even Uwa's colleagues teased her about it before they all departed and went to their various homes. But not before Solomon took Uwa's number. Solomon's warm and engaging attitude drew her in, and it was clear that they'd had more than just a casual talk. Their meeting in the pub would signal the start of a new chapter in Uwa's life, as the chance contact with Solomon paved the way for a new and exciting relationship.

Solomon's outstanding looks were difficult to overlook; he was tall and attractive, and he exuded a dominating presence that drew attention wherever he went. His powerful physique and athleticism added to his charm, conveying a sense of confidence and energy. Aside from his physical characteristics, Solomon's voice was mesmerising. It had a deep, resonant tone that resembled a melodic song, both manly and relaxing. His voice had the ability to captivate and hold people's attention, much like a memorable song. Uwa was drawn not only to Solomon's physical appearance, but also to the charm and charisma he radiated. Uwa was also drawn to Solomon because he shared the same faith as hers; they were both Christians and could talk bible, church and everything else.

Solomon and Uwa soon quickly became a pair and went everywhere together. Everyone called them the golden couple; they both made a match that radiated peace and harmony. Solomon met Uwa's children, and Uwa also met his two children from a previous relationship.

On a cold evening in April, Uwa and Solomon had just returned from watching a movie and were sitting in Solomon's car. Uwa was going to say good night and get into her car to drive home, but Solomon stopped her. "Uwa," he began, his voice tinged with emotion, "I've watched you and listened to your stories of how you have been through life's highs and lows with grace and resilience. Your strength has inspired me in ways I can't fully express. I like the way you love God and your trust in Him to see you through everything," Solomon continued. Uwa's heart quickened, curious about the purpose behind Solomon's words. "You are a remarkable woman, Uwa," Solomon continued. "Your dedication to your children, your unwavering support for your friends, your faith and connection with God, and your strength in facing life's challenges, it's all awe-inspiring." Uwa listened intently, her eyes filled with curiosity and anticipation as Solomon's words painted a picture of admiration and respect. But in her heart she was saying, *Get on with it, Solomon, and stop repeating yourself.* "But beyond that," Solomon said, his tone softening, "I've come to realise that in every glance, every smile, and every shared moment, there's a bond that's grown between us. Uwa, I've found something incredibly special in you, something I can't imagine my life without."

Solomon then dipped his hands into his pocket and took out a little, nicely wrapped box. He looked into Uwa's eyes, his own shining with sincerity. "Uwa, will you make me the happiest man in the world? Will you marry me?"

The air seemed to quiet as Uwa's eyes opened in surprise and delight. Tears streamed from the corners of her eyes as she realised the gravity of the situation. Her heart filled with a mix of emotions, including elation, astonishment, and a strong sense of being loved. Uwa nodded, overcome with emotion. "Yes, Solomon. Yes, I will." Uwa never expected this to happen; after all, she and Solomon had only known each other for about six months.

Solomon's eyes shone with delight as he carefully grabbed her hand and placed the ring on her finger. Uwa returned home delighted and singing praises to God all the way. Her choruses had many meanings for her; some she sung in gratitude to God, others with grief in her heart, and how she had trusted God and now he had answered her prayers by bringing a man into her life whom she loved and wanted to marry. She was happy. She also loved that Solomon got along well with Anne and Benjamin. Eager to share her joy, she quickly reached for her phone, her fingers bouncing across the screen as she dialled her mother's digits.

"Mom!" Uwa shouted, her voice full of joy when her mother answered the phone. "I have the most incredible news to share. Solomon just proposed, and I said yes! We're engaged!"

Uwa's mother was ecstatic, her voice ringing with happiness and love on the other end of the phone. "Oh, my dear! I'm thrilled for you. Congratulations! Solomon is a wonderful man, and I couldn't be happier for both of you." Uwa had spoken to her mum several times about Solomon in the last six months. "This is fantastic news!" Her mum burst into a song of praise in her native Agenebode language. Uwa's heart filled with warmth as she imagined her mother's reaction. She could practically feel the lively energy through the phone, picturing her mother's ecstatic celebration, a dance that usually preceded moments of joy and thankfulness in their family. She envisioned her mother, a beauty of grace and excitement, breaking out into the traditional dance she used to show her delight, celebrating the good news with a joyful rhythm. The mental image evoked feelings of nostalgia and familiarity, bringing back recollections of special family events and joyous occasions.

Aunty B was the next person Uwa wanted to tell about her wonderful news, so she called her right away. Aunty B, who had been a constant source of support, answered the phone with her usual kindness. "Aunty B, you won't believe it," Uwa exclaimed, her voice bursting with excitement. "Solomon proposed, and I'm engaged!"

Aunty B's happy laughter rang across the phone. "Oh, my dear, that's wonderful news! Congratulations, Uwa. I'm so happy for you. Solomon is a gem, and I wish you both a lifetime of happiness together."

During the passionate talk with Aunty B, Uwa spotted her phone indicating an incoming call. She looked at the screen and realised it was Solomon calling. Excitement and expectation flowed within her as she spoke to Aunty B.

"Sorry, Aunty B," Uwa replied with a twinkle in her eyes. "I've got to take this call from Solomon; I'll talk to you soon!"

Aunty B, realising what was happening, expressed her delight once more at Uwa's engagement. "Absolutely, my dear! Go ahead. Congratulations again! Talk to you soon."

With a short goodbye, Uwa quickly switched the connection, her heart bursting with delight and adoration as she replied, "Solomon!"

Solomon's excitement was obvious as he spoke. "Uwa, I couldn't wait to hear your voice. I'm overjoyed and I can't stop thinking about our future together. Are you home yet?"

Uwa's heart swelled with ecstasy at his words. "I feel the same way, Solomon. This is truly a lovely occasion for us; I'll be home soon." Solomon assured Uwa of his love and promised to call her back for a quick goodnight conversation before they went to bed.

Following the ecstatic engagement, each day was a painting of wedding ideas and gorgeous chaos. Uwa found herself caught up in a tornado of preparations, turning her days into a joyful frenzy of decisions and dreams. Uwa was lost in a world of possibilities, from choosing her wedding gown, which would weave memories into its delicate fabric, to designing the beautiful decorations that would grace their celebration. She sifted through bridal magazines and boutiques, looking for the right outfit to make her feel like a vision of love and happiness on her special day.

The careful curation of the menu became a focus, with talks centred on the combination of flavours and culinary delights that would captivate the guests and leave an indelible impression. Uwa and Solomon indulged in tasting sessions, savouring the foods that would commemorate their blissful union. Every arrangement, flower accent colour, and item of décor had to capture the essence of their love story. She relished in the planning process, finding satisfaction in every decision she made, knowing that each detail would contribute to the beauty and sentiment of their wedding day. The procedure, while sometimes daunting, was a monument to her and Solomon's love for one another and the celebration that awaited them, a celebration that would mark the start of their journey together.

Finally, the wedding day arrived, and Uwa and Solomon stood together in front of the church, their eyes full with excitement and expectation. The small, intimate gathering of friends and relatives had arrived to witness their wedding. The preacher, a lovely and kind man, began the ceremony with a friendly smile. As he discussed love, commitment, and the journey of marriage, Uwa and Solomon exchanged meaningful vows, promising to support and adore each other for the rest of their lives. Uwa's vow to Solomon was a pledge she had read in the Bible, where Ruth promised her mother-in-law, Naomi. This vow is found in the Book of Ruth, specifically in Ruth 1:16-17 (NIV): "But Ruth replied, 'Don't urge me to leave you or to turn back from you. Where you go, I will go, and where you stay, I will stay. Your people will be my people, and your God my God. Where you die, I will die, and there I will be buried. May the Lord deal with me, be it ever so severely, if even death separates you and me.'" Uwa saw Ruth's vow to Naomi as a moving illustration of the dedication and commitment that could be found in a loving and enduring marriage, in which two people promise to stand by each other's side and share their lives through all situations. This was the type of marriage she envisioned for herself and Solomon. Solomon and Uwa were no longer young in age but they had each had previous marriages, relationships, and children; putting everything together to be successful was critical for Uwa.

On that wedding day, Uwa and Solomon exchanged vows in front of their friends and fellow churchgoers, who knew this was going to be something special. The church's mellow, golden light provided a warm and inviting ambiance, enhancing the sense of reverence and oneness. As the minister called them husband and wife, Uwa and Solomon exchanged their first kiss as a married couple. The church exploded with applause, and happy laughter filled the air. Following the wedding, the church courtyard was transformed into a lovely garden banquet, where the newlyweds shared their love with their loved ones. It was a day full of joy, love, and faith, and Uwa and Solomon could not have hoped for a better start to their married life. Uwa's parents were not able to attend the wedding. This was because Uwa's mother was ill and in the hospital; Uwa was not informed beforehand of the gravity of her mum's illness because her family did not want to spoil her joy at remarrying knowing what she had gone through with and after Joe's death.

The reception was a brilliant tapestry of colours, sounds, and flavours. Tables were adorned with exquisite Nigerian foods such as jollof rice, fried rice, different types of meat, chicken and fish, dodo, suya, efo riro, Ogbono soup and egusi soup as well as a variety of delectable deserts. The smell of spicy grilled meats permeated the air as laughing and lively discussions echoed across the area. Uwa, the gorgeous bride, couldn't resist the allure of the dancefloor. She was known for her contagious love of dancing, and tonight was no exception. The music, a combination of traditional Nigerian rhythms (Afrobeats), Christian music and modern hits, drew her to the heart of the dance floor.

Uwa swirled and swayed in her magnificent bridal gown while her guests applauded and cheered. Solomon, the groom, joined her on the dance floor, and they moved in perfect sync, their smiles revealing their great affection for one another. The night appeared to go on forever, with the stars overhead watching Uwa's energetic and joyful dancing. As the hours went, more and more people joined in, and the party grew into a stunning event.

Following the wedding, Uwa and Solomon moved into a new home that could accommodate Solomon, Uwa, and Uwa's two children, Anne and Benjamin, as well as Solomon's children when they visited. Weekdays were filled with activities. Uwa would help Anne with her schooling, and their laughter and shared moments strengthened their friendship. Meanwhile, Benjamin and Solomon were frequently caught up in lengthy sports debates, and they watched football games together, each rooting for their favourite team. However, the true magic occurred on weekends and during holiday seasons. Solomon's children from his former marriage, Sarah and Daniel, would pay him a visit. The house would come alive with the sounds of youthful joy, and the children would embrace each other as if they had always been siblings.

On Saturday afternoons, they would all assemble in the backyard for a picnic, with the makeshift football pitch serving as a battleground for laughing and friendly rivalry. Anne and Sarah would create an inseparable friendship, sharing secrets and dreams late into the night, while Benjamin and Daniel would wander into the woods behind the house, backpacks in hand and eyes full of adventure. Holidays were a special time for adventure and discovery. Uwa and Solomon would plan visits to new areas, leaving lasting memories for the whole family. Uwa had just the life she had always wished and prayed to God for.

Chapter 7 – Not Again...

Despite the family's happiness and peace, considering this was a blended family who had overcome societal discouragements, Uwa occasionally noticed how Solomon would sometimes sit alone, looking lost and deep in thought. Many such times she would pray to God to heal him from whatever it was that troubled him. In her calm nature, she would just sit beside him to show comfort and her availability to share his thoughts with her. Other times she would ask him what the matter was, but he would always say nothing. His famous line was, "My baby, there is nothing to tell and nothing to worry about." As much as Uwa did not like this response, there was nothing she could do. With each passing day, Uwa became more and more concerned about Solomon. He appeared more and more withdrawn and she wondered what the issue might be. Solomon had a nice job which paid a good wage and had loads of perks, he had a good relationship with his children, he spoke to his family and friends and life appeared good. She knew she had been a dutiful wife and had not done anything to warrant him being unhappy. Uwa thought they were fine, but there was clearly an issue somewhere. She also noted that Solomon was not attending church as frequently. He would make excuses; he was simply different from how he used to be.

One day, Uwa's eyes were filled with deep anxiety as she looked at Solomon, her beloved husband. She couldn't bear to see him like this, and she enquired, "My darling husband, I see you are sad. What is troubling you?"

Solomon, as he often did, initially brushed off her inquiry, but responded more harshly than he would normally do with, "Leave it, nothing to talk about." But with Uwa's persistence, Solomon reluctantly began to speak, his words laden with sadness. "Uwa, there's something I've never shared with you: about five years ago, I was deeply in love with a certain lady called Lola; we were so close, so in love, and we even made plans to marry." Uwa's eyes widened with surprise, knowing the seriousness of the story her husband was about to tell. Solomon continued, his voice filled with sadness. "But then, a terrible twist of fate shattered our dreams: she was deported back to Nigeria because she didn't have the necessary immigration papers to stay in the UK." Immigration officials came to her place of work, discovered she was working with a fake document, and deported her because she couldn't provide her resident permit to work and live in the UK. Uwa's heart wrenched for Solomon, so she stretched out to hug him, offering him comfort and compassion, but Solomon gently removed her hands from across his shoulders.

Solomon continued. "After Lola's deportation, I never heard from her again; it was as if she had vanished from the face of the earth and my world, leaving behind a void that I tried but couldn't fill." He paused for a time, reminiscing those painful years. "And then, just three months ago," his story went, "I got a phone call from an old friend of mine who knew about our relationship back then. I was surprised to learn from him that he had seen Lola in East London and she asked about me. My friend said he told her I was fine and now married, but she gave him her number and insisted that he gave me the number and said I must call her as it was rather urgent and important. My friend said Lola said she had returned to the UK about a year ago and ever since then she has been looking for me or someone who knows me. She was happy to have seen my friend that day. My friend said he struggled with giving me the number but due to the urgency in her voice and face when he saw Lola he had no choice but to tell me."

Solomon continued. "My dear wife, Uwa, at that stage I wanted to tell you but as I had never mentioned my relationship with Lola to you in the past, I changed my mind. However, I made the call."

Solomon proceeded to narrate the details of the call.

"Hello, Lola, this is Solomon speaking."

Lola says, "Hello?"

Solomon: "I'm very glad to speak with you; what happened? How did you disappear?"

Lola: "It's fantastic to hear from you, too! Unfortunately, the day I was deported, I initially tried to run and, in the process, lost my phone. I was however still caught and sent back to Nigeria. I tried to recollect your number off head but could not and that was why and how I lost contact with you."

Solomon replied, "That makes sense now. Those days were horrible for me not knowing exactly what happened to you." He explained that he was now married to Uwa and that they had four children, two from his previous relationship which Lola knew about and two from Uwa's previous relationship. Solomon said he told Lola that he was very happy and all that was left that would really make him happy was for Uwa to have a baby for him. Solomon said he longed to be a dad again as he was never fully in his children's lives due to the divorce from their mother.

Lola expressed her happiness that Solomon had moved on, and she revealed that she had had a terrible few years too. Lola proceeded to tell Solomon that when she was deported and arrived in Nigeria, she discovered she was pregnant after a few weeks, and of course the pregnancy was for Solomon. Solomon was astonished by Lola's news.

Lola went on. "I'm feeling better; it was a difficult time, but life has a way of teaching us important lessons. Regarding the pregnancy, I opted to keep the child. It hasn't been easy, but our daughter has been a source of joy in my life." She said she was able to get a scholarship to come back to the UK with their daughter. Lola went on to tell Solomon that she had named their daughter Grace, after Solomon's mother. Grace was now about three years old and looked just like Solomon. Lola said she tried her hardest to find Solomon when she found out she was pregnant, and she searched for him every day of her life even after she returned to the UK.

Solomon continued and revealed to Uwa that after Lola's news, he had gone to their house to meet with his daughter Grace. Uwa had always considered her marriage to be strong and built on trust, and the revelation that her husband had been calling and visiting another woman left her feeling completely shattered. She couldn't fathom why he had kept this secret from her for so long. Tears welled up in her eyes as she confronted him, her voice trembling with a mixture of anger and hurt.

Uwa asked, "Solomon, how could you do this to us? How could you have kept all of this from me? I believed we had a strong and honest relationship."

Solomon was visibly startled by her reaction; he had not imagined the extent of the anguish his acts would cause. "Uwa, I can't explain why I did what I did. I never intended to hurt you. It is a mistake I sincerely regret. I'm very sorry."

Uwa was also shocked to hear Solomon say that he felt their family was incomplete because Uwa had not had a baby. Solomon had never once mentioned to her that he wanted them to have a baby; she had completely taken that part of bearing children in marriage for granted. She loved her husband deeply, but her trust had been shattered, and she didn't know what to do next, but as a godly woman, she decided to support him. This baby was already here and would be a part of their family.

The revelation about Solomon's past and the unexpected return of the lady he had once loved had a profound impact on their marriage. In the weeks and months that followed, their relationship underwent a transformation. Solomon changed in ways that Uwa could not have anticipated. He became increasingly preoccupied with his past, and it seemed as though the weight of unresolved emotions and unanswered questions was taking a toll on him. Solomon's routine began to revolve around visits to his children. He would frequently go to see Sarah, Daniel, and Grace, but none of them ever came to their house again. The once lively and joyful atmosphere that had characterized their family gatherings had faded, replaced by an air of tension and uncertainty. Uwa watched as her husband became distant. It felt as though a wedge had been driven between their once harmonious family life, and she yearned for the way things had been before. Despite the challenges they faced, Uwa remained steadfast in her love for Solomon. She was determined to stand by him, no matter what the future held. It was a testing time for their marriage, one that would require patience, understanding, and communication to navigate the changes and uncertainties that had now become a part of their lives.

 The changes in Solomon's behaviour became increasingly difficult for Uwa to bear. He returned home late, frequently ignoring her calls and text messages. The stillness and distance between them grew, and Uwa felt increasingly isolated and frustrated. It was evident that something had changed in their marriage, and the unsaid tension weighed heavy in the air. Uwa's concern for her marriage and her husband's behaviour prompted her to seek support from her parents, Solomon's parents, and their pastor. They all cared profoundly about Uwa's and Solomon's well-being and attempted to intervene in the hopes of assisting the pair in overcoming their difficulties. Despite the support and efforts of those who cared about their relationship, the distance between Uwa and Solomon continued to grow. Conversations were held, and Solomon promised to change, acknowledging the pain he had caused.

Unfortunately, his words did not translate into actions, and the situation became increasingly difficult for Uwa to bear.

The day came when Solomon, in a solemn and sincere talk with Uwa, declared his plan to end their marriage. They sat down for a meeting, and he revealed his choice with a heavy heart. "Uwa," he began, "I've been doing a lot of soul-searching, and I need to be honest with you. I've taken the painful decision to end our marriage." He paused for a while, staring into her eyes with a mix of sorrow and sadness. "I want to go back to Lola so we can both raise Grace together." When Uwa heard these words, tears welled up in her eyes. She had readied herself for the possibility, but the reality was heartbreaking. Her marriage, once full of hope and love, was now coming to an end. Solomon went on: "I'm sorry, Uwa. I know this is painful, but Lola and I have a child together, and I feel a responsibility to be there for Grace. After all, we haven't been able to have children together."

Uwa nodded. Her voice was shaking when she replied, "I understand, Solomon. This is an incredibly difficult decision, and I appreciate your honesty. It's just... it's painful, and it's going to take time for me to come to terms with it."

Uwa's heart fell the next day as she entered their home when she came back from work, only to find it empty and devoid of the presence that had been a part of her life. Solomon had walked out, leaving her with only a note and the keys to their house. With shaky hands, she took the note and read the passionate but devastating words. "I am sorry. Please find it in your heart to forgive me." The words resonated in her head, a vivid reminder of the love they'd previously shared and the tremendous sorrow she now felt. Uwa's eyes welled up with tears as she realised that the chapter of her life centred on Solomon had come to an end. She was left to deal with the room's emptiness, the weight of his absence, and the difficult process of healing and moving on that lay ahead. Uwa realised that forgiving would take time, and the agony of this unexpected departure would leave scars on her heart. But as she stood in the silent chamber, she felt she had the strength to reconstruct her life, find happiness again, and chart a new route forward.

Uwa's world had disintegrated in the aftermath of Solomon's sudden departure. The sorrow and the turmoil that surrounded her rendered her incapable of performing even the most basic of activities. She couldn't eat, and self-care, such as taking a bath, seemed like an impossible task. Her grief was so deep that she considered suicide in order to escape the awful torment. However, the love and duty she felt for her children became her lifeline. Her trust in God, too, gave her hope and the strength to persevere, even at the darkest of times. Once again, she relapsed and had to be restarted on anti-depressants as she had stopped taking them about a year ago under the guidance of her doctor.

Uwa understood she needed support to get through this extremely tough phase in her life. She went out with friends, relatives, and her pastor, sharing her sorrow and seeking comfort. Through their love and support, as well as her unshakeable faith, she gradually began the long and difficult process of healing and rebuilding her life, for her own sake and the sake of her children. The weight of losing two men, each in their own way, felt unbearable. In the quiet of her weeping, she cried out to God, her faith shaken but strong.

"Why me?" she sobbed, the question ringing across her empty bedroom. "First, my husband passed away, and now my second husband has left me. Why, God?"

The agony she felt was indescribable, the sense of loss and abandonment too hard to take. In her prayers and tears, Uwa sought explanation, solace, and a gleam of hope in the middle of her sorrow.

The impact of Uwa and Solomon's breakup extended beyond Uwa. Her children, Anne and Benjamin, were also deeply affected by it. Worse, Solomon did not answer her calls and had blocked them. She spoke with his mother, who stated she didn't know what to do but urged Uwa to forgive him and advised her to move on with her life. Uwa's marriage vows came flooding back to her, but they now held no meaning. She wondered how long Solomon's mother, who had always been supportive, had known about Lola and Grace. Uwa couldn't tell her mother much about how she felt because she was still quite ill. Uwa had no idea of the extent of her mother's illness because she lived in Nigeria; her siblings and father only told her that she was getting better. They had heard from Uwa about what had happened in her marriage and did not want to put pressure on her.

A few months later, Uwa's sister during one of their phone conversations advised strongly that she needed to come to Nigeria to see their ill mother. Even though Uwa's sister did not reveal much more than that, Uwa sensed this was not good and she immediately made plans to go see her mum in Nigeria.

Uwa's voyage to Lagos was marked by a heavy heart, and her visit to her mother's hospital ward was both emotional and heartbreaking. As she entered the room, her gaze landed on her mother, who lay in a hospital bed, her once-vibrant spirit dimmed by her sickness, Her mother appeared fragile and weak, in sharp contrast to the powerful and elegant woman she had always known. Uwa's emotions overcame her, and she had to leave the room to hide her tears. It was almost unbearable to see her dear mother in such a situation. She remembered all the times of courage, love, and care her mother had given her throughout her life, and it was difficult to see her suffer. Uwa forced herself to calm down and returned to the room to be with her mother.

Uwa and her siblings and dad all sat with Uwa's mum and now and again everyone would each hold her, and speak words of comfort and assurance, pledging to be there for their mother throughout this difficult time. The path ahead was bound to be difficult, but Uwa was determined to provide her mother the same love and care she had received her entire life. This was even more difficult for Uwa as it brought back memories of the time she had cared for Joe when he was sick too.

The night at the hospital with her mother was a mix of sadness and treasured moments spent together. Uwa never left her mother's side, providing comfort and solace as best she could. Early one morning about five days after Uwa came to Nigeria, as she sat with her mum in her hospital room, the doctor came in to see Uwa and her mum. Uwa was advised by the doctor to contact her father and siblings, to come to the hospital for a meeting. Uwa had asked her dad and siblings to go home and rest as she felt they had been the ones taking care of their mum all these while and she could support, they had only left a few hours ago. Uwa called her sister and relayed the message that the doctor suggested the whole family come into the hospital for a meeting. In less than an hour, they all gathered around her mother's bedside and the doctor delivered the terrible diagnosis. Only a few days remained for her adored mother. The weight of this discovery was great, and everyone in the room burst into tears. In the midst of their collective loss, they clutched onto one another, finding strength in the familial relationships that had always provided support and love.

Uwa and her family spent the next few days with their mum. A few days later, their mum, who hardly spoke due to pain and her ill condition, spoke and as her strength faded, with a feeble but loving voice, she muttered, "I love you all, and may God be with you always." After which she passed away. Her family took comfort in knowing that she was now at peace, surrounded by her family's love and God's presence.

In the days and weeks that followed, Uwa and her family were saddened by their tremendous loss, but the memory of those last words was a reminder of the enduring love that would always be a part of their lives.

Uwa's heart was sad as she left Nigeria and returned to the UK a few days after her mother died. The sadness of her loss weighed on her, but she knew there were plans to be made and responsibilities to fulfil, even from afar. Over the next month, Uwa and her two children, Anne and Benjamin, planned to return to Nigeria for her mother's burial. They gathered their strength and made the appropriate travel arrangements, knowing that they needed to be present to wish their loving mother and grandma farewell.

The voyage back to Nigeria a second time was fraught with mixed feelings, both sombre and full of memories of their mother and grandmother's love and the glorious times they had experienced. The funeral was a moving tribute to a full life, a celebration of their mother's love and legacy. Uwa, Anne, and Benjamin took comfort in being surrounded by relatives and friends during this trying time. The event served as a reminder of the value of joining together as a community during times of loss and grief, as well as providing them with a sense of closure and the opportunity to say their final goodbyes.

Uwa's mother's funeral was a celebration of a full life and a testimony to her legacy as a woman of tremendous faith and love. Family, friends, and members of the community came together to pay their respects and honour her memory. The atmosphere was one of remembrance rather than sadness, with anecdotes and recollections shared that highlighted her unshakeable devotion to God as well as her commitment to her family and community. The service included hymns, prayers, and words of memory that reflected the enormous impact she'd had on people who knew her.

The focus of the service stayed on her love, generosity, and spiritual advice to others. It was a lovely homage to a woman who had left an indelible impression on the hearts of many. As they laid her to rest, there was a sense of closure, knowing that her spirit and the ideals she established in her family would continue.

Uwa and her children returned home to the UK a few weeks later from her mother's burial to an unexpected and unpleasant revelation. Among the messages and letters she received was a divorce letter from Solomon. The timing of this letter, coming so soon after her mother's death, exacerbated Uwa's overpowering sense of loss and instability. The divorce letter served as a sharp reminder of the changes and difficulties that had arisen in her marriage, and it marked the formal end of their partnership. Uwa's heart, already heavy from her mother's death, was further burdened by the weight of this letter, leaving her with a tremendous sense of loss and anxiety about her future.

Uwa found the next days to be very difficult. She had to deal with both her mother's death and the terrible process of divorce. She remained strong, however, due to her unshakeable faith and the support of her loved ones. She was a woman who overcame adversity with grace and strength, but she had a deep revelation that stood out in her mind: "the one that makes you happy can also make you cry." What a life. Solomon made her happy but now made her cry, a deep difference to how she ever imagined her life would be.

Chapter 8 – Please, Sir, Don't Die

Uwa used her pain to embrace her work, faith, and love of charity. She said to herself daily, "I have no choice but to be happy and being happy depends on me." She knew Solomon was not coming back. Uwa engaged in women's groups, where she discussed her personal experiences and encouraged and supported others who had endured similar challenges. Her experience of overcoming misfortune, including widowhood, divorce, and separation served as a source of hope and inspiration for others. She demonstrated that even in the midst of life's most terrible challenges, it was possible to not only survive but also thrive. Uwa felt that she needed to do this as her role of motherhood was not as active as it used to be.

Benjamin and Anne had grown older, and they basically now did their own things. She was a proud mother seeing her children do well. In her quiet moments, she would say to herself, "God, I thank you that even though marriage did not work for me, motherhood did." Uwa had a sense of humour that she used to support herself when she felt low in mood. Benjamin was now in his final year of university studying electrical engineering while Anne was in her first year studying nursing. Uwa was happy that love, advice, and support she had given them throughout the years had paid off. However, Uwa, being in her "empty nest" stage of life, needed to fill the void of her children's laughter and the void in her heart. Therefore, she decided to focus on her own development and interests. While it brought with it a sense of loss and nostalgia, it also offered up new opportunities and allowed her to rediscover herself as a person outside of her duty as a mother. It was a time for

Uwa to focus on herself and discover new prospects and passions as she looked ahead to the future. One such adventure was travelling.

Travelling was something Uwa had always wanted to do but had been unable to pursue fully due to her motherhood duties. Uwa in her travels discovered a strong feeling of pleasure in seeing new places, experiencing diverse cultures, and making experiences that were all her own. The world became her playground, and each location carried with it the thrill of adventure and exploration. Sometimes Uwa would travel alone; other times she would travel with other ladies. Either way, it was always fun.

During one of her trips to Spain, Uwa met Dare. He was older, divorced, and shared Uwa's love of travel. He was a large man who stood pretty tall. Their mutual enthusiasm in discovering new locations and experiencing the world drew them together in an unexpected way. They met four days before Uwa was scheduled to return home. During those few days, they became good friends and shared stories, meals, and laughter together. Unfortunately, the holidays came to end. They exchanged numbers and kept in touch. Soon they were having regular phone conversations and messages, but one thing was missing. They needed to see each other again in order to understand exactly what the relationship meant. Dare lived in Nigeria, and Uwa lived in the United Kingdom, so they therefore decided to meet in a neutral and mutually beneficial location where they could spend quality time together and get to know each other better.

Uwa's decision to meet Dare in a neutral nation and explore the possibilities of their relationship was unquestionably significant. It was normal for her to be concerned about her future and the idea of starting another relationship. In times of doubt and uncertainty, she opened her heart to God, expressing her doubts and fears and asking for His wisdom and guidance in this new chapter of her life.

Dare and Uwa decided to meet in Morocco. They would be able to visit the country's lively cities, sample its great cuisine, and immerse themselves in its diverse history and landscapes. Dare arrived a day earlier, ready and enthusiastic for the approaching meeting. Uwa had a range of mixed feelings in the hours running up to her trip to Morocco, including excitement and a touch of worry. As the day of her departure arrived, she packed her things and caught her flight, and four short hours later she arrived at Agadir Morocco airport as her pulse raced with excitement and anticipation. When she saw Dare waiting for her, a broad smile spread across her face, and she jumped into his outstretched arms without hesitation. Uwa was overjoyed to see him, but something struck her immediately. He was considerably larger in stature than she remembered. As Uwa and Dare approached a taxi, Uwa noticed Dare's heavy breathing. She glanced at him, concerned, as he began to breathe more heavily, and it became clear that he was battling for air. Uwa was overcome with worry and panic as she realised Dare was struggling to breathe. She asked whether he was all right, but he was unable to respond, and Uwa realised that quick medical attention was required.

Without hesitation, she called for help and sought assistance from others nearby. Their first goal was to get Dare the medical attention he needed, as his well-being was of the utmost importance. A taxi quickly helped Uwa take Dare to the nearest hospital. As Dare was brought to the hospital, Uwa's heart was filled with anxiety and fear. She couldn't stop crying as she sat by his side. She reached out to him, her voice shaking with passion, and said repeatedly, "Please, sir, don't die." "Please, sir, don't die." "Please, sir, don't die." The words were a desperate appeal, a heartfelt cry for the man she had just recently reconnected with. Uwa could not believe that life was having an impact on her yet again. As she sat at Dare's side in the hospital, her life seemed to rush before her eyes. The worry and uncertainty of the scenario were overwhelming, and she couldn't help but imagine the stories and judgements that would be made about her decision to meet a stranger in a distant nation. She was concerned about what others would say or think about her activities, thinking they might misinterpret her motives or her connection with Dare. As Uwa sat in the hospital, her mind was filled with fear. The potential of Dare's death loomed huge in her mind, and it was too agonising to consider. The weight of her previous losses, including the death of her mother and the dissolution of her former marriage, contributed to the load she carried. In her anguish, she cried and shook her head, seeking comfort and fortitude to face whatever came next. She uttered a passionate prayer to God, asking for divine intervention and direction. She implored with tears in her eyes, "Please, God, heal Dare and see him through this." Dare started feeling better two days after his health scare and hospitalisation. The fog of worry that had hung over Uwa and Dare began to lift, leaving behind a glimmer of hope and comfort.

Dare's recovery was a positive turn of events, and Uwa's prayers had been answered. God was good. As he began to feel better, their shared moments were filled with appreciation and a recognition of how delicate and valuable life can be. Dare's doctors diagnosed him with a number of health issues, including high blood pressure, diabetes, and obesity, all of which might have a substantial impact on his well-being. It was a wake-up call that emphasised the significance of taking care of his health and making the required lifestyle modifications. Dare would need to start losing weight and adopt healthier behaviours in order to improve his health and overall quality of life. This would entail changing his diet, increasing his physical activity, and carefully managing his medical issues with medication and regular check-ups. Uwa and Dare's time together in Morocco was filled with a variety of emotions and experiences. Following Dare's recuperation and departure from the hospital, they spent a few days together, each in their own hotel room, reflecting about their relationship and the routes they intended to take.

Despite their strong bond, Uwa decided not to pursue a romantic relationship with Dare. She had solid reasons for making her decision, including the geographical distance between them, her own need to heal from previous relationships and traumas, and her worry for Dare's continued health journey. Uwa discussed her decision with Dare, who understood and respected her point of view. They bid goodbye with mutual understanding and a commitment to stay in touch. It was a farewell defined by respect and concern for one another's well-being.

Uwa's return to the UK just in time for Christmas was a poignant and joyful reunion with her two children, Anne and Benjamin. The holiday season offered a sense of unity and family bonding, and they treasured the memories they created. Christmas was a time of love, laughter, and celebration, made even more memorable by the presence of Uwa and her children. They decorated the house, exchanged gifts, and ate holiday dinners together. Uwa, Anne, and Benjamin found time to sit together, gazing at old photographs and talking about their father, Joe, whom they truly missed. Sharing stories and experiences helped them keep Joe's memory alive in their hearts and minds.

Chapter 9 – You Called Me What?

Uwa learnt that life includes ups and downs, and she must remain steady in her faith no matter what she was going through. She often told herself that God had been wonderful to her since she knew that without Him, things would have been far worse. She knew that better days were on the way, and that God was on her side. Uwa was a humorous person with a way with words, and she would often come up with proverbs she had heard elders say while growing up in Nigeria. One such adage was, "Someone wey don see 99, 100 no go be new thing." This stated that no matter what life threw at her, she would always rise above it. Another one was, "Wahala no dey finish but God dey run am make better things happen to him pickin'."

Uwa would regularly ask herself who actually in this world was fighting for her, and she would answer just GOD. She refused to see herself as a failure of have self-pity. But gradually over time she had learnt to start to trust others, one of which was her friend Adaora. Adaora was someone Uwa had known for many years. They had laughed, grieved, and exchanged secrets that they believed would be kept secure. Uwa had spoken up to Adaora about her relationship troubles. These discussions were therapeutic, providing a sense of release as she unburdened her soul.

Adaora was aware of guys who would approach Uwa for dates. Uwa would always seek her advice on whether to date or not, and they would almost always agree that none of Uwa's suitors were qualified to be with her. Uwa travelled extensively with Adaora, and they operated several programmes to assist women in their community. Adaora herself had three young sons. She'd left Nigeria for the United Kingdom a few years ago in search of better opportunities. However, her split from her husband was an unanticipated stumbling block on her journey. Her husband had stayed in Nigeria due to professional responsibilities, and this geographical difference, despite Adaora's dreams for a better life in the UK, proved to be a considerable emotional and practical challenge. She found herself juggling the obligations of raising three sons alone while dealing with the emotional strain of being separated from her spouse. Her attempts to urge him to join them in the UK were received with reluctance as he appeared steadfast in his choice to stay in Nigeria.

Uwa and Adaora, both lonely ladies, found refuge in each other. Uwa was careful not to visit Adaora too frequently since she had not forgotten what Nkechi once taught her: a friend in need is a bloody nuisance. Thinking about this now made Uwa laugh but she remembered it was not funny at all at the time. Uwa, on the other hand, was well aware that she was no longer seeking relief from human beings, but rather from God. As Uwa and Adaora spent more time together, Uwa became increasingly uncomfortable with their interactions. Adaora's attitude began to show signs of insecurity and judgement, especially when they were in public. Uwa never wanted to believe that Adaora was jealous of her. Adaora regularly made references to Uwa's expensive clothes, jewellery, bags, and shoes. She would comment on the nice car Uwa drove and how she loved to always do her hair and nails frequently with "Na wa for this Uwa sef she can like to dress".

Uwa had also noticed how during their outings, Adaora would comment on how guys seemed to pay more attention to Uwa, alleging they stared at her more and approached her for her contact information while seemingly ignoring Adaora herself. This cycle of comparison and perceived attention developed jealousy and animosity in Adaora, which influenced their relationship. Uwa became increasingly uneasy as these remarks underlined Adaora's insecurities. She tried to grasp Adaora's point of view, recognising the underlying fears that could have caused such behaviours. However, Uwa found it difficult to confront the problem because Adaora's actions continued to impair their relationship. Uwa always reminded Adaora however that she was married and asked if she wanted to cheat on her husband.

One day, as they sipped tea and spoke about relationships in Uwa's cosy living room, Adaora spat a harsh remark. "You know, Uwa, with all your failed marriages and being a widow, people in this neighbourhood call you a prostitute. They say you can't keep a man, and that's why you've been through so much." The words hung heavy in the air, like a stinging, unexpected slap to Uwa's face. She was stunned to silence. Uwa's initial reaction was a combination of shock, dismay, and great disbelief. The anguish from Adaora's harsh words hit deep, rekindling emotions Uwa had experienced in previous failed relationships. The statement "not again, another friend" lingered in Uwa's head, suggesting a sombre understanding of a painful pattern. In the midst of the shock and anguish, Uwa felt a sense of guarded resignation—a realisation that this unpleasant incident was, sadly, not new to her. The buddy she had trusted had used her challenges and vulnerabilities to harm her. Uwa's eyes welled up with tears as she struggled to comprehend Adaora's harsh accusation. She had expressed her experiences and anxieties with the hope of finding empathy and understanding, not being branded in such a negative way. "Why would you say that, Adaora?" Uwa managed to murmur. "I believed I could trust you with my emotions; I thought you were my friend. You called me what? You are using the secrets I have told you to pass such unfounded comments on me, calling a prostitute," Uwa continued.

Adaora's expression revealed no remorse as she continued. "I'm only telling you what people say. You should be more cautious about who you open yourself to, including me even," Adaora said. Uwa believed in the power of honesty and the beauty of unguarded connections with others, and she had always taken pride in her openness and simplicity. Being authentic meant baring her soul, offering an unfiltered view of her thoughts and emotions. Uwa however never really told others her main stories except during counselling and women's conferences when she would lead by the holy spirit and use her stories and what had happened in her life to encourage others. However, Adaora's words had awakened a realisation within her: the quality of authenticity she cherished most about herself might not be as ideal as she'd once believed. The purity of being an open book suddenly felt tarnished. The exposure of her innermost self to the world left her feeling naked and defenceless.

Adaora's departure was as sudden as her unexpected revelation. She suddenly picked her bag, hissed, and walked out of Uwa's house. The silence that followed her exit was almost deafening. Uwa stood there, thinking about the unexpected betrayal that had just unfolded. Uwa's heart was softened by her innate kindness and compassion, and as she settled into the solitude of her room, she found solace in the serenity of her nightly prayers. In the stillness of the night, Uwa clasped her hands and closed her eyes, seeking guidance and peace. Her prayers were not only for herself, but also for Adaora. Uwa awoke the next morning with a determined spirit, ready to embrace the new day. Her pursuit of happiness wasn't just a personal endeavour; it was a mission she carried with grace and purpose. Being labelled the "Happiness Queen" by her friends was more than just a title; it reflected her commitment to spreading joy and contentment in the lives of those around her. Uwa realised that happiness was more than just the absence of difficulties, but also the ability to discover joy in the middle of them. The weight of the betrayal and the unexpected departure of a close friend had taken a toll on her spirit, gradually seeping into her daily life. Despite her best efforts to maintain her positive demeanour, the emotional burden had become too heavy to bear. Uwa knew she was in no state to go to work that day.

Uwa decided to report her absence from work to her manager, as well as to seek help from her GP, in her journey to healing. She also decided to seek solace in prayer, and her faith in God was a deeply personal and meaningful choice. Uwa also made a decision to go for Christian counselling in order to help her come to terms with all she had been through.

She sat down in her home office and wrote out a prayer to God, a prayer for God to heal her mental health:

Dear God.

I come to You with a heavy heart, seeking your comfort and strength in the midst of this difficult journey I find myself on. The weight of depression has enveloped me, and I feel lost in its darkness. I ask for Your healing touch, O Lord, and I surrender my pain and burdens to You, knowing that You are the ultimate healer and the source of all comfort. You know the depths of my struggle and the shadows that cloud my mind. Please, God, grant me the strength to face each

Lord, guide me through this journey of healing; grant me the resilience to overcome the challenges and the faith to believe in the promise of brighter days ahead. Help me to find the strength to face each moment, to seek support from those around me, and to trust in Your divine plan for my life. May Your peace, which surpasses all understanding, envelop me, bringing a sense of calm amidst the storm. Let Your love be a beacon of hope that guides me out of this darkness.

Uwa printed this prayer off and started to say it at any given opportunity she had every day. She would also add other words as they came up in her prayer time. She would add scriptures and often stay silent at the end of her prayer session to hear from God.

Uwa came to a profound realization that the depression she faced wasn't solely a consequence of Adaora's betrayal but rather a culmination of the weight of the challenges she had carried for years. It was as if the accumulation of burdens had finally reached a breaking point. In this moment of clarity, Uwa made a conscious decision to surrender these burdens to Jesus. She realized that she couldn't carry the weight of these challenges alone anymore. With a heart heavy with the accumulated pains and adversities, she gave them all to Jesus, finding solace in the promise of His love and guidance. She understood that she didn't need to face these challenges alone.

Uwa felt seen, understood, and uplifted by the unwavering love and encouragement of her church family, children, friends, and her beloved Aunt B. Their presence became the pillars that held her up during her darkest moments, providing a constant source of comfort and reassurance, serving as a healing balm to her wounded spirit. As the days passed, she felt a newfound sense of resilience and hope blossoming within her, and she gradually resumed her normal activities, feeling a sense of familiarity and comfort in her routine once again.

She returned to work after being off sick for nearly three weeks. Uwa attended Christian counselling. Her losses and strengths were discussed, and the pain over the years was listened to and validated. Christian counselling provided a source of revelation to Uwa, a revelation that she could use to make solid changes in her life. It was based on God's word, blending the wisdom of the mind with the strength of the Spirit, where faith and psychology were used to aid healing and recovery. Uwa found comfort in the soft but strong direction counselling provided. Her counsellor reminded her of her value and the love of a God who had never left her side, even in her worst circumstances. Every session brought fresh insight as she worked to let the bitterness go that she had been clinging on to unknown to her, pardon others and herself, and welcome the freedom forgiveness offered. Her counsellor gave her useful coping mechanisms for her loss, therefore enabling her to negotiate the complicated feelings that sometimes returned. They cooperated to establish limits in her relationships, therefore enabling her to guard her heart while also accepting love and relationship. The bits of her life started to fit together slowly. She found strength she never knew she possessed, happiness long buried, and peace more profound than comprehension.

Chapter 10 – A Journey of Self-Discovery

One day, Uwa woke up feeling a sensation she could not fully describe or understand, but she went on to start praising God and said, "This is the day the Lord has made, and I will rejoice in it and be glad." Uwa felt that there was nothing that could come her way anymore in life that could affect her as deeply as all the things that she had been through in her life. She remembered her husband's death, her mother's death, her divorce, several betrayals, her mental health issues and much more. She gave God the glory that despite it all, she was still standing. Uwa remembered the sermon that her pastor had delivered on the Sunday gone. A message where he had encouraged the church to be steadfast in the Lord and trust God with all their heart even in times of trials. Uwa grinned and said, "I will trust in God and rejoice always." She knew that it was the Holy Spirit that was working in her from her inside and making her feel calm and relaxed. The counselling had definitely helped her reconnect with her real authentic self. She felt free meditating on the love of God as she lay in bed for a minute, and there and then she decided to once again lay all her burdens at the feet of Jesus. Suddenly Uwa felt relief on her shoulders, as if a great weight had been lifted. She suddenly felt the urge to pray, but it was not the normal prayer. Uwa got up from her bed and knelt by her bedside, raising her hands in total surrender to God. Uwa made a new commitment to God, and promised to always say yes to his will and his ways and worship him. Uwa felt confidence, strength, and direction pouring over her with every word she said. She was praying not only for herself but also for the knowledge to negotiate obstacles in life and to inspire hope and optimism for others.

She prayed loudly, "I refuse to have mental health issues," and she kept in her prayers handing every element of her life to God. She then stopped reading to listen to her Lord and Saviour and enjoy the warmth of his embrace. Uwa grasped for her Bible, heart full of fresh spiritual vitality. Turning the pages, she came upon the narrative of the woman with the issue of blood for twelve years. She read, "Just then a woman who had endured for twelve years with continual bleeding walked up behind him. She felt at the edge of his robe, thinking, 'If I can just touch his robe, I will be healed.' Turning around, Jesus remarked, 'Daughter, be encouraged!' as he spotted her. 'Your faith has healed you.' And at that instant the woman was healed." (Matthews 9:20–22). Before she understood God was speaking to her, Uwa did not have to venture beyond verse 22. She imagined the scene: the packed streets, the woman's desperation, and her firm conviction that simply touching the hem of Jesus' garment might cause a miracle recovery. Uwa could relate with this story as she noticed similarities between her own life and that of the woman in the Bible story account as she became engrossed in the story. Uwa had battled her own hardships and times of hopelessness, just as the woman had experienced problems and roadblocks. Knowing that health and transformation were not unattainable, Uwa, too, had a comparable surge of faith inside her, much as the woman who reached out in faith did.

After her prayers and reading of the scripture, Uwa sat in her preferred armchair and thought about her children, Benjamin and Anne. The years that passed had turned them into self-sufficient individuals carving their own courses in life. She had lost sight of who she was outside of that position as she had committed so much of herself to being a loving mother. Now on a foreign ground—the lack of continuous motherly responsibilities—she was at a junction. Uwa resolved to see that this phase of her life presented a chance for personal growth. She came to see she could pursue fresh interests, pick up old pastimes, and explore unexplored ground that had been neglected during her years of committed parenting.

The following weekend, Uwa was all alone at home and she began a reflective journey considering a question that lurked deep in her mind—"Who am I?" She said aloud, "I am a daughter of the Kind, God's own delight, a child of Mercy. Knowing it was time to get Grace, she viewed herself in a different way and not just as a mother or identifiers the world used but as a lady of God, someone God has chosen. She understood that none of her difficulties defined her and all she was and had been from God.

She said to herself, "I am a synthesis of my experiences, beliefs, desires, and aspirations, but I am sure not the names and identities humans have put on me—a widow, a single mum, a divorcee, the one whose husband left her, a prostitute, a this or that. I am a daughter of the highest GOD"

"I AM GOD'S DELIGHT".

Uwa consciously decided to start a path of self-expression in search of rediscovery. She understood that sometimes, originating from internal changes she desired to bring about in her life, transformation starts with the exterior altering her presentation of herself to the public. She went to the hairdresser with a fresh sense of direction and selected a haircut that said volumes about her yearning for transformation. She felt a load off her shoulders the minute the scissors cut away her long hair. The new haircut was a statement of a fresh chapter in her life, and not only about appearance.

She then had to consider her clothes. Uwa dug through her wardrobe, separating the clothes that had felt more like an obligation than a statement of who she was. She assembled pieces that spoke to her soul bit by bit. She selected clothing that reflected her changing identity and made her feel confident, secure, She accepted a look that reflected her real self, free from social conventions or expectations. She wore vivid hues that matched her newly discovered vitality some days and more muted tones that matched her reflective attitude other days. The key was that every decision she made reflected her changing path. She owned them. Not out of vanity but rather as a means of self-respect and self-care, Uwa started to pay more attention to her appearance.

Driven by her fresh sense of self and goals, Uwa set out to match her career to her personal ambitions. She admitted that her employment had to give not only financial stability but also the freedom to follow her interests. Having a definite idea in mind, she started looking at chances that would allow her the time and room to foster her entrepreneurial energy. Understanding that this would be a spur for her dreams, Uwa sought jobs with flexibility—perhaps remote work or flexible times. She changed her résumé and started networking, interacting with people and groups matched with her interests.

Uwa also moved yet again to a new house, which represented a metaphorical change in her life. It was a literal mirror of the fresh start she was embracing, not only a change of address. She found the freedom and solace in this new environment to foster her work on her dreams and talents. Uwa also returned to university working on her master's degree in business administration. This choice represented a turning point in her pursuit of personal development and her goals to increase her business-related expertise. She soon graduated and was so pleased with herself that she'd got through the difficulties involved. Her master's degree was more than simply a degree; it was a stepping stone towards realising her goals and significantly impacting the commercial and entrepreneurial landscape.

Uwa also decided start writing as she opened a brand-new page in her e- note book, as that enabled her write and not type straight from her heart. Every word spun her experiences, knowledge, and dreams into a story that would uplift and empower others. Her spirit spilt over the pages, her narrative turning into a lighthouse of resiliency and hope.

Uwa's participation in ministry also became more deep as it developed into a dynamic and influential commitment. Her commitment to helping the women's arm of her church was not only a duty but also a calling she accepted totally. She gave women in the community direction, compassion, and encouragement so they could find comfort in their faith. Assuming a leadership role, she oversaw prayer sessions at other fellowships as well as at her church. Her administrative services to the church guaranteed efficiency and organisation, therefore guaranteeing that the spiritual home operated well and could thus meet the requirements of its members.

Uwa's preaching became a pillar of enlightenment and spiritual development in the mid-week seminars. Her style combined the story of her own resiliency with biblical lessons. Emphasising the value of faith and the relentless support she discovered in her relationship with God, she related her own path. Her Bible teachings went beyond simply scripture teachings to show how faith may be a lighthouse helping one negotiate personal challenges and hardship.

Understanding the worth of days spent with her children, Uwa also made it a point of duty to connect with Benjamin and Anne. She loved the memories she created. They would all often travel around Europe on trips to discover the beauty of different cities, and she made it a point to build lifelong memories with them. These common excursions turned into fun and bonding opportunities that strengthened their family links. Benjamin's life had changed when he discovered love with a stunning lady; their relationship was blossoming and they were considering marriage. Benjamin was now 25 years old and he one day told his mum that he wanted to propose to his girlfriend, and Uwa was delighted. Anne was 23 years old now and she had graduated and was working as a community nurse in a local hospital near where she lived. Anne and Benjamin no longer lived at home with Uwa, which was one of the reasons she had moved to a small, cosy two-bedroom apartment. As her children developed on their own paths, she stayed a guiding presence providing her knowledge, love, and encouragement.

Uwa's unflinching faith stayed rock solid, her constant source of strength. Her faith in God helped her to negotiate the highs and lows of her life. Her confidence in God became the cornerstone around which she constructed her life, therefore forming her values, behaviour, and perspective. Her life had turned into a rich and interesting colour. Uwa found great satisfaction in her fresh sense of direction, family, education, her objectives in ministry, her efforts in both her personal and professional life. She found gratification that went beyond any depressed or gloomy mood. She welcomed every day with thanks, delight in the small joys, comfort in her faith, and direction in her work. And gradually Uwa never felt low in mood, depressed or anxious again.

Chapter 11 – Rekindling Love

Uwa had been deeply immersed in her journey of self-discovery and personal growth. Her first book she was writing was exciting; however, she felt she needed some skills to be able to do this well. She attended a workshop on a fine Saturday afternoon that focused on various aspects of writing, including characters that need to be developed in the book, plot structuring, and the intricacies of editing. The event provided valuable insights into the journey of crafting a book, featuring talks by established authors, writing coaches, and publishing experts.

As Uwa engaged in conversation with a publisher, eager to gather information about the publishing process for her future book, she found herself immersed in a dialogue about the intricate world of book publishing. However, amid her discussion, she encountered a man also in conversation with publishers, discussing his own publishing requirements. The man appeared amiable and engaged in the publishing industry. With a warm smile, he introduced himself as Martin, an experienced writer who had published several books in the past. Their conversation effortlessly transitioned from casual introductions to a discussion about their writing journeys. The chance encounter at the conference not only provided Uwa with valuable information on the publishing process but also unexpectedly resulted in a budding friendship with Martin, someone who shared similar dreams and aspirations in the world of literature. He asked for her number as she left, escorting her to her car. Uwa left the conference feeling inspired and equipped with a wealth of knowledge to further her aspirations in writing.

Later that evening, Martin called to ensure Uwa had arrived home safely after the eventful day at the conference. During their exchange, he casually mentioned his plans to attend church the following day, which happened to be a Sunday. Curious about Uwa's religious affiliation and practices, Martin politely inquired if she identified as a Christian and whether she regularly attended church services. Uwa appreciated Martin's considerate gesture in checking on her well-being and, in response to his inquiry, shared that she indeed identified as a Christian. She expressed her belief in the Christian faith and told him that she would also be attending her church the next day. Their conversation smoothly transitioned into a discussion about their faith, experiences, and the role it played in their lives. They shared personal stories and reflections on how their beliefs influenced their daily activities, including their work, relationships, and personal growth. The exchange about faith and personal beliefs not only highlighted a common ground between Uwa and Martin but also paved the way for a deeper and more meaningful conversation beyond their initial acquaintance.

They ended the conversation that night with Martin asking Uwa if it was OK for him to call the next day, and Uwa said yes. True to his promise, Martin called the following day, and Uwa, in agreement with their plan from the previous night, happily received his call. Their conversation was warm and engaging, with topics ranging from their respective work lives to their shared hobbies and, notably, their passion for writing books. Martin shared insights about his professional life, describing the challenges and rewards of his work. Uwa reciprocated by discussing her own career endeavours, exchanging anecdotes about her experiences and the projects she was involved in.

As their conversations became a regular and cherished part of their daily routine, Martin found himself increasingly drawn to Uwa's engaging personality, wit, and shared interests. With their growing connection and a desire to spend more time together, Martin eventually asked Uwa out on a dinner date. He suggested a cozy restaurant known for its delightful ambiance and exquisite cuisine, hoping to take their friendship to the next level. Uwa, pleasantly surprised by the invitation, appreciated the thought and enthusiasm behind Martin's proposal. Her fondness for their conversations and the growing connection made the idea of meeting in person quite appealing. With a genuine smile in her voice, she agreed to the dinner date, looking forward to the opportunity to finally meet face-to-face and spend more time together beyond their daily phone conversations.

Uwa felt a mix of emotions as the anticipated dinner date drew closer. Despite enjoying her conversations and growing connection with Martin, she held a level of scepticism and caution, reminding herself that she sought only friendship at this point in her life. The idea of a romantic relationship felt a bit daunting, prompting her to approach the upcoming meeting with an emphasis on preserving their friendship.

Uwa arrived at the restaurant with a blend of excitement and apprehension. During their dinner, their discussions were as engaging and enjoyable as their phone conversations. The evening was filled with laughter, stories, and shared interests. Uwa found herself appreciating Martin's company, enjoying the camaraderie and feeling grateful for their blossoming friendship.

After a few successful dates and numerous engaging phone conversations, Uwa felt comfortable extending an invitation to Martin for a church event. During one of their conversations, Uwa mentioned an upcoming church programme, expressing her enthusiasm for the event. Given their growing friendship, she extended an invitation to Martin, inviting him to join her at the church service or event. Martin, open-minded and respectful of Uwa's beliefs, accepted the invitation graciously. He saw this as an opportunity to explore and understand a part of Uwa's life that was important to her. He admired Uwa's commitment to her faith and was genuinely interested in learning more about this aspect of her life.

On the day of the church event, Uwa and Martin arrived together, greeted warmly by members of the congregation. Uwa felt a sense of joy having Martin by her side, sharing a part of her world that held significant meaning to her. Throughout the service or programme, they listened to the sermon, participated in the activities, and shared in the fellowship of the church community. The experience not only allowed Martin to gain insight into Uwa's faith and values but also further solidified their bond as friends. They shared meaningful conversations about the sermon and the overall experience, deepening their understanding of each other's perspectives and beliefs.

Following their shared experiences and growing closeness, Martin found himself developing deeper feelings for Uwa. Acknowledging their strong bond and the compatibility they shared, he felt ready to take their relationship to a more serious level. In a heartfelt conversation, Martin expressed his genuine emotions to Uwa, admitting that he cherished their connection and valued her as not just as a friend but as someone he could envision a future with. He conveyed his desire to formally commit to a romantic relationship and work together towards building a future that he hoped would culminate in marriage. Despite her initial reservations about starting a romantic relationship, she valued their friendship and the connection they had built. She acknowledged her own growing affection for Martin and the potential of their bond evolving into something more profound. After considering her feelings and the strong connection they shared, Uwa decided to take a leap of faith, agreeing to embark on a romantic journey with Martin. Both understood the significance of the decision and were committed to nurturing their relationship, aiming to build a solid foundation based on love, respect, and shared values. They both agreed to build this putting God at the centre of it all. Uwa felt she had made so many mistakes regarding relationships and this time she wanted to do it right, starting it with God and following Godly biblical principles about courtship and marriage. Uwa shared her different experiences with Martin about her first and second marriages, her pain of widowhood and divorce. He in turn had been married once and was now divorced. He felt happy that Uwa trusted him enough to tell him such details. They always ended their discussions with prayers for a better future, trusting God that their relationship would end in praise.

Having been through a divorce, Martin knew the depths of personal challenges and the transformative power of faith in overcoming adversity. His experience shaped his understanding of resilience and compassion, allowing him to connect deeply with others who faced similar trials. With four adult children, all married and with families of their own, Martin had experienced the joys and complexities of parenthood. He held family values close to his heart, cherishing the moments spent with his children and grandchildren while fostering a strong sense of unity within his family. Uwa found a kindred spirit in Martin.

In a moment filled with deep emotion and a shared commitment to their faith and aspirations, Martin soon proposed to Uwa during a romantic dinner. With sincerity and a deep sense of respect for Uwa and her family, Martin also took the traditional and heartfelt step of reaching out to everyone important in Uwa's life. He spoke to her father, siblings, children, aunt, friends, and her pastor, expressing his genuine love and desire to marry Uwa.

Uwa and Martin's decision to attend marriage counselling with their pastor as Martin had decided to fellowship in Uwa's church so they could worship in the same place. Following the counselling sessions, Uwa and Martin celebrated their love and union in a traditional Nigerian wedding ceremony, which they flew to Nigeria to have. This beautiful cultural celebration included the payment of the bride price, which was a significant custom in Nigerian weddings, symbolizing respect, honour, and the joining of two families.

Subsequently, Uwa and Martin chose to have a simple and intimate wedding ceremony to further bless and celebrate their union. This more private event allowed them to exchange vows, expressing their love and commitment in the presence of their closest family and friends.

After the wedding, Uwa moved into Martin's house and she dedicated herself to transforming their home into a warm and welcoming place. She invested time and effort into decorating, meticulously choosing paintings, decorations, and furniture to infuse the house with her personal style and create a space that reflected their combined tastes. The furniture arrangement was also a significant part of Uwa's effort to create a comfortable and functional living space. She combined her and Martin's preferences, ensuring that the furniture not only looked aesthetically pleasing but also provided practicality and comfort.

As Martin and Uwa settled into their daily routine, they found comfort and joy in the simple pleasures of family life. After their workdays, they looked forward to spending their evenings together, creating a cozy and intimate atmosphere within their home. Their evenings were a blend of shared activities that reflected their interests and values. They often started by winding down while watching movies, which allowed them to relax and enjoy each other's company. In addition to their leisure activities, they valued spiritual connection and made it a habit to read the Bible and pray together. This shared devotion helped strengthen their bond and provided them with a sense of unity and tranquillity before retiring for the night.

Martin's passion for cooking led to delightful evenings filled with the aroma of delicious meals. He particularly enjoyed preparing English and Mediterranean dishes, utilising his culinary skills to create flavourful and diverse meals for their dinner. Uwa, in turn, showcased her culinary expertise by preparing traditional Nigerian dishes, infusing their home with the rich flavours and aromas. Weekends became a cherished time for them, offering opportunities to relax, engage in activities that strengthened their bond, and explore shared interests. They dedicated some weekends to attending conferences, where they could enhance their knowledge, network, and explore new ideas together. Their commitment to faith remained an integral part of their lives. They regularly attended church services, finding solace and spiritual nourishment in their shared faith. It was a time for them to come together, partake in communal worship, and connect with their spiritual beliefs. They served in their church and had other fellowships they belonged to where they supported others.

Travel became another focal point of their shared experiences. Martin and Uwa ventured to different destinations, exploring new cultures, cuisines, and sights. In addition to their outings and travels, they also devoted time to visit and spend quality moments with their combined six adult children. Benjamin and Anne worked in very good jobs in big cities in the UK. Martin had four children and was even a grandfather with five grandchildren. He had two sons and two daughters. They all loved Uwa just as Uwa's two children loved Martin. Martin and Uwa had a real focus on fostering a sense of unity and warmth within their extended family. Whether through family gatherings, dinners, or other activities, they aimed to create a strong and supportive family network that embraced their union.

Martin and Uwa made sure they sowed a seed of trusting in the lord in their children and always made sure they led them back to biblical principles anytime they came to them for advice. The six children always valued and listened to all advice offered.

Martin would regularly say that his motto was from the words of an old hymn titled "What a Friend We Have in Jesus" and he would say the phrase in the hymn that says, "What needless pains we suffer when we do not carry our needs to God in prayer." He stood by those words and told Uwa at every given opportunity, "Uwa, my dear wife, never forget the privilege to invite God to everything that concerns you, both great and small."

Uwa and Martin prayed together daily but would always find time daily to spend in their own quiet time in prayers and scripture reading. They never took each other for granted. Their love was built solidly on God's words and Christian principles.

Chapter 12 – God Has the Final Say

Uwa watched as Martin slept. She always enjoyed listening to his breathing and how his face looked like that of a baby when he slept. She began to pray, thanking God for seeing them through the last ten years of marriage. She could not believe that it was ten years ago she and Martin tied the knot. She finally had begun to know that this one was destined by God and no more would she suffer any issues around marriage. She said to herself, "I have finally entered my new dawn and indeed God had the final say."

She expressed her thanks to God that she had embarked on a new phase in her life, characterized by positivity, hope, and a sense of renewal. This was so because she sometimes doubted secretly that Martin would not one day leave her, as she remembered all her bitter experiences with marriage and relationships. Occasionally she wondered where Solomon was. The last she heard, he had moved back to Africa after he had done a DNA test with Grace and found out that Grace was not his biological child. She had been informed about this by a mutual friend. The story was soon after Solomon had moved in with Lola. They started to argue all the time about Lola not being a true Christian, always going to parties and staying out till late in the night every weekend and spending money lavishly which she did not have but did so using credit cards, with the bills coming back to him to pay. It was during one of these arguments that Lola had voiced out that Grace was not his child. Solomon then decided to secretly conduct a DNA test, which confirmed that indeed he was not the father of Grace. Soon after, Solomon told Lola his findings and moved out of their home and eventually moved back to Nigeria. Uwa felt sad for him but all she could do was offer a word of prayer to God for him. She never heard from Mehmet, Abbey, Rob or Dare. She did wish she could see Mehmet again though as he was really a good friend. She heard also from mutual friends that both Nkechi and Adaora were divorced. Nkechi's husband ended the marriage due to the continuous fights she had with his mother, while Adaora's husband ended the marriage because he caught her cheating during a visit he'd paid to London without her knowing he was coming to town. Uwa smiled to herself and said, "Now who is the prostitute?" God had been faithful. She once again thanked God for bringing Martin into her life. God had the final say. He only can do great things in a person's life.

As she continued to ponder in her thoughts, Martin stirred in bed and said, "Good morning, my Queen, and happy wedding anniversary to us." He turned and gave her a big kiss and warm embrace. They held hands and prayed together, as they did every morning. After the prayers, Martin told Uwa how much he loved her and thanked her for being his wife. He said he was taking Uwa out for a special day to celebrate.

THE END

www.ingramcontent.com/pod-product-compliance
Lightning Source LLC
Chambersburg PA
CBHW050304120526
44590CB00016B/2486